MARK

MARK

THE BEGINNING OF THE GOSPEL OF JESUS CHRIST, THE SON OF GOD
MARK 1:1

JOHN METCALFE

THE PUBLISHING TRUST
CHURCH ROAD, TYLERS GREEN, PENN, BUCKINGHAMSHIRE.

Printed and Published by
John Metcalfe Publishing Trust
Church Road, Tylers Green
Penn, Buckinghamshire

—

Distributed by Trust Representatives
and Agents world-wide

In the Far East

Bethany, Orchard Point P.O. Box 0373
Singapore 912313

—

—

First Published May 1996

—

ISBN 1 870039 70 X

—

CONTENTS

INTRODUCTION

MARK

INTRODUCTION

THE paramount importance of all four gospels can never be overstressed. Nor can the importance of considering each account separately. Neither is it possible to over-emphasize the necessity of balancing the presentation of each evangelist side by side, so that the Spirit's fourfold witness to the testimony of Jesus is seen in proportion. There is no other way to view the whole gospel aright.

To over-emphasize one gospel at the expense of another is to distort the reflection of Jesus mirrored to perfection in the glass of the fourfold truth given by the Holy Ghost.

To 'harmonize' the gospels together into one so-called 'life' of Jesus—as many have attempted to do—achieves nothing other than to clash into horrendous discord the already perfect harmony of the fourfold testimony of the Holy Ghost to the greatness of Christ.

Such meddling corrupts the perfection of the balance of scripture. It elevates the high-mindedness of the flesh above the mind of the Spirit. It shatters the glorious image of Christ presented in fourfold harmony. And it defiantly challenges the witness of the Father from heaven to the chosen apostles: 'This is my beloved Son: hear him.'

But where can one hear him? Nowhere other than in the testimony of this selfsame apostolic witness, each in its proper proportionate and relative place of balance: Matthew, Mark, Luke, and John.

Perfect dimension, exquisite poise, and consummate fulness lie in the fourfold witness of the gospels. This infallible representation of the testimony of Jesus has been achieved by the Holy Ghost in the distinct but parallel records of Matthew, Mark, Luke, and John, so that a finely balanced perspective appears to those who seek the knowledge of Christ and would reiterate the question, 'Sir, we would see Jesus'.

If so, it is essential to focus upon the pure word of God—in edition and version—in itself for oneself. This becomes the more imperative in the light of the prophetic parables of Matthew thirteen, where the corruption at the close of this present age is viewed as being worse than that during the last days of the Jews.

Those were the times in which the Jews crucified the Messiah, blasphemed the Holy Ghost, rejected the testimony of God, and, as a nation, turned with one accord from the gospel.

Therefore in coming to the word of God today it must be borne in mind continually that the decline, failure, and final apostasy of which Jesus then prophesied, has now come upon us. A corruption more or less, in one degree or another, reflected in the literature presented under the guise of helping us in the scriptures.

Hence wisdom lies in returning with a broken and contrite spirit, trembling at his word, with great self-distrust, in penitent humility going back past all books, histories, and traditions to Christ and his apostles, opening that only safe word on bended knees in the secret closet. 'And thy Father which seeth in secret shall reward thee openly.'

For we are warned of the interpretations under which men have buried the scriptures. Denying their traditions, we ought to come with the scriptures and a broken heart into the presence of the living God, remembering the Father's voice which came from the excellent glory, heard by the apostles in the holy mount. This is the voice to which we give attendance.

But let none say that we despise to learn from others. We do not despise to learn from those who have learned of God. But we abhor the chaff put out by those who have learned of man, whose doctrine comes from no higher elevation than the shelves of their own miscellaneous libraries.

From such bookworms we neither can nor will learn. Void of the presence of the living God, unconscious of the interior teaching of Christ, and destitute of the leading of the Spirit into all truth, these at their very best but regurgitate the dead letter in consequence of their paper gobbling forays.

In Christ's words, it is not bread, but a stone that they offer. It is not fish but a serpent which they provide. For an egg, they give a scorpion. And what living soul can bear this miserable diet of the clerics? They are full of carnal reasonings, worldly speculations, and airy diversions. In consequence, they are forever blowing out clouds of dusty chaff, which quite prevents the breathing of the quickened children of God.

But the secret, hidden, and interior ministry of Christ from heaven at once gives bread, not a stone; offers fish, not a serpent; provides egg, not a scorpion. Christ gives heavenly light, spiritual doctrine, and divine teaching, breathing upon us and saying, 'Receive ye the Holy Ghost'.

Far from chaff, Christ administers the bread of life. Instead of blowing the stifling dust of death from the grave, he imparts the breath of life from the glory, quickening us into life. And who would exchange this ministry for any other?

Those who have learned of the Father, come to Christ alone. The sheep hear his voice and follow him. But the voice of a stranger will they not hear, neither will they follow strangers.

Hirelings are a proven disaster to the flock of the Good Shepherd. But he who shows his sheep the path of life has spoken, and their ears have heard his divine breathing, just as their eyes have seen the heavenly vision. In the mount of the LORD it shall be seen: 'This is my beloved Son: hear him.'

Who would resist wholly giving himself to hear him whose words are spirit, they are life? who has the words of eternal life? who leads us within even now in spirit to the heavenly places in glory, to the Father, in whose presence is fulness of joy, and at whose right hand are pleasures for evermore?

We can learn from none other: Who teacheth like him? Certainly not the earthy, dead ministries of carnal men, full of academic speculation and clerical presumption.

But we know that *we* know nothing; and we know that *they* know nothing either. We turn from our own ability; and we

turn from theirs also. For to us there is but one God, the
Father, of whom are all things, and we in him; and one Lord
Jesus Christ, by whom are all things, and we by him.

And if so, we must—we can do no other—we must turn to
him, crying, 'Lord, to whom shall we go? *thou* hast the words of
eternal life'. Then it is to him only—revealed in the gospels—
that we turn, and not to another.

And the spiritual, used to such things by experience, know
that this is of God. Because it is *direct* from God. It is to them,
as it is to us, spiritual food. So then, we will learn of those
men, and those only, whom God *himself* has approved.

Moreover, we will not merely *read* them, but in the power
of Christ, do the things which he has said by them, obeying
their spiritual direction for ourselves in our own day, led by
the voice of him that speaketh from heaven. Thus we will have
this ministry *live*, quickened from above, and not generations
dead.

But, whether dead or alive, few and far between are those
ministers who have learned of Christ, being taught by the
Spirit. And of those few, all too many have been at once half
of one sort and half of another. This confuses the sheep.

Therefore the spiritual must learn to distinguish sharply
between what is of God and what is of man, even in the writings
and sayings of those who appear to be called of Christ. Everything must be tested by the anointing, lest any be led beyond
what is edifying and spiritual to embrace what is perplexing
and carnal, because both come from the same pen.

This is Christ's own teaching, namely, 'Take heed how ye
hear'. And again, 'Take heed what ye hear.' Finally: 'Take
heed that no man deceive you.' And these admonitions were
never more pointed than in the interpretation of the gospels.

To interpret the four gospels, two mysteries must be opened. The first of these is the vision of Christ unique to each evangelist. That is, the concept of every gospel in turn. It is essential to understand that a distinctive view of Christ exists, peculiar to each one of these four books.

Hence a fourfold vision is presented to convey the whole, because all four facets are essential to the complete revelation of Christ, though each is integral and unique within itself. The question here is, What is the Concept of Mark?

The second mystery to be opened in the divine interpretation of the gospels is the way in which the vision or concept is unfolded, namely, the spiritual flow of the chapters and verses which constitute the sum of each one of the gospels. This is the narrative itself, comprising the arrangement and argument of the events and discourses that make up the distinctiveness of each particular evangelist.

These chapters and verses, respectively, are unique, inviolable, and peculiar to the integrity of each singular gospel. The question follows, What is the Argument of the text in Mark? what is its Structure, unfolding from the first verse of the first chapter to the last verse of the last chapter?

PART ONE

THE CONCEPT OF MARK

THE CONCEPT OF MARK

HERE the term Concept refers to the distinctive way in which Mark reveals Christ. This is something that has been lost beneath the traditions of interpretation from past generations, and, at the present time, lies neglected and unsought under the prevailing apathy.

Reaching back into the mists of previous ages and ancient traditions, characteristically Christ has been represented—or rather misrepresented—in the gospel according to Mark by the almost universal interpretation that he appears as the Servant. That is, with virtually unbroken monotony, tradition has it that Mark presents Jesus as the Servant of God.

Such a traditional concept almost certainly finds its hoary origin in the fanciful and allegorical imaginings of the — so-called—'fathers'. In fact, these were the fathers of that apostasy which followed soon after the death of the apostles.

These 'fathers' have been 'canonized' wholesale by the Roman Catholic system: the more 'saints' the better. And yet they never had anything other than speculative fantasy to commend them. Thus 'The Church' has buried them beneath layers of antiquity—like so many lichen covered fossils—as if this warranted obligatory veneration throughout all generations.

No sooner had the apostasy spread universally after the death of the apostles, than the 'fathers' gained the ascendancy. From that point onwards ignorance and superstition reigned. Plain truth became more and more obscured by being 'spiritualized', and, in consequence, the traditionally scholastic interpretations of successive blind leaders of the blind became the rule.

Noticing that the mystical 'living creatures' in the visions of Ezekiel were four in number, these pestilential 'fathers' fancifully supposed—with total disregard to proportion, comparison, and logic—that, there being four gospels, the four living creatures must therefore signify Matthew, Mark, Luke, and John.

But what creature signified which gospel? Superstition, the light of which is darkness, attended by ignorance, the spur of which is presumption, acted out the ludicrous farce of matching creature to gospel. And what conjuring tricks must inevitably follow, given no higher motive than to justify the asinine speculation that any correspondence—between 'creature' and gospel—existed in the first place?

Thus their fancy roved: There were four living creatures, Ezekiel 1:5, but 'their appearance was the likeness of a man'. Ergo, the man Christ Jesus in all the gospels.

But if one Christ in all the gospels, Why four gospels? Um; yes: Why? Ah, observed these fathers of all divinity faculties and clerical traditions, 'As for the likeness of their faces, they four had the face of a man, and the face of a lion, on the right side: and they four had the face of an ox on the left side; they four also had the face of an eagle', Ezekiel 1:10.

To such wildly imaginative 'fathers' the problem was solved. Just as the appearance of a man common to all indicated Christ in the sum of the gospels, so the distinct fourfold faces possessed by each showed the vision or concept of Christ held respectively by Matthew, Mark, Luke, and John. Oh, yes? Then why *all* four faces common to *all* four creatures, instead of *one* face peculiar to each *one* of the four?

Again, the fact that the *appearance* of a man was common to *all* the living creatures, yet the *countenance* of a man was also duplicated in one of each of their fourfold faces, posed no problem to these blind leaders of the blind. You see that all logic and intelligence must necessarily be abandoned by those who enter the portals of their so-called 'Church'.

That is, every sound rule of exegesis, or even plain common sense, must be abandoned in favour of abject subjection. A subjection necessarily mingled with the feigned adoration of relics, idols, and 'saints'; a subjection played out in the mock humility of gesture, posture, and payment; and, of course, a subjection cowed by deadly fear of the papist custodians of this disgusting parody of the Christian religion and its apostolic doctrine.

Ignoring the inconvenient fact that *all four faces* belonged to *each and every one* of the four creatures — then, *to all four gospels!* — the learned doctors preferred oblivion in order to concentrate upon the problem of *which* face fitted *what* gospel. Here was a question quite beyond the laity. It was a question eluding even the clergy. This was a matter exclusive to the profound collegiate of professors.

Into conclave the learned body must go; into retreat the sainted academics must pass: meanwhile both church and state, breathless, must await their final and—of course—unquestioned pontification.

Had we been enabled to enter their deliberations, it is pretty certain that we would have discovered them to have begun with this absurdity: the Eagle was John.

But countering their fancies, I ask, Why? John the Eagle? Did the other evangelists lack wings? Because from no less puerile a whim than that the eagle flew, and flew high and alone, they pontificated, That is John.

Then what were the other evangelists? Earthbound burrowers? Come to that, if John should be the eagle *because* he flew high and alone, why are the eagles' *faces* mentioned, but *not* their wings?

Again, since *each and every one* of the living creatures had wings *in and of themselves*—'And *every one* had four wings', Ezekiel 1:6—then by *those* wings each one with his respective *four faces* was equally elevated—four faces and all—and possessed the same heavenly flight as the other, the eagle neither more nor less than the ox.

Further observe that to these inept and bungling 'fathers', the fact that not so much as the *word* 'eagle' occurs in John is irrelevant. *They* had spoken. Then what on earth gave *John* the right to disturb their cogitations?

To avoid being disturbed by any further such distractions, they shut their eyes tightly against the clear and lucid truth that both Matthew and Luke *do* mention eagles. Oh, but we must submit, not question; we must listen, not think. The papistically canonized 'fathers' had spoken: and, in their view—and that of 'The Church'—all mortal flesh must keep silence.

Of course, John does mention a flying eagle in Revelation 4:7. But then, that was *distinct* from the Lamb upon the throne, not *representative* of him. Besides, it just happens that we *were* discussing the gospels, not the Revelation.

However with blithe disregard to all reason, the 'fathers' next ascribe the face of a man to Luke. As though the manhood of Christ quite eluded the grasp of Matthew, Mark, and John! As though the four creatures had not the likeness of a man in common! As though each of the creatures were not equally possessed of the face of a man just as much as its fellows!

Nevertheless the imprimatur had been stamped: Luke was the Man from that time henceforth. 'The Church' had spoken. But in truth, it was no more than that the asses had brayed.

Left with two gospels and two faces, no doubt our erudite scholars, breathing a sigh of relief, would feel the exegetical victory to be at least fifty per cent within their grasp. Let us see, they must have agonised: Mark and Matthew; a lion's face and that of an ox; Whichever shall we put together?

Although we *do* find oxen in both Luke and John, inconveniently these 'fathers' had already used up *those* gospels in their previous hallucinations. Not that they would have noticed, but actually *neither* ox *nor* lion is mentioned in either of the two gospels awaiting their chosen designation.

Refusing to be outdone, perhaps after tortuous discursive ramblings on the part of these schoolmen, one can imagine a somnolent voice intoning from the sepulchral depths of some armchair in the shadows: 'Well; well; there *was* a certain lion of the tribe of Judah.'

The straw is clutched: Matthew is the Lion. But no lion, much less of the tribe of Judah, appears in Matthew. Yet despite every *fact* staring them full in the face, still they opt for Matthew being the gospel signified by the face of a lion.

Now nothing remains but the inevitable. What had they left? One gospel; one face. Ergo: Mark is signified by the Ox. The ox portrays labour. Labour denotes service. Ergo, Christ is the Servant in Mark.

13

Thus it was determined. The thing was established. They had spoken. And it was written. And who is so old or wise, or who has such antiquity, as these fathers? Who? Why, Satan, the father of lies, of course.

And, though the origins be lost from sight, from this dark ignorance, this crass blindness, this benighted superstition, the tradition has continued to this day.

This has been carried through the Reformation, unbroken, to modern commentaries, to evangelical heroes, yet to be reiterated even by those who claim to have forsaken traditions, and to know better, such as J.N. Darby, J.B. Stoney, and other chief men and writers among the Brethren.

How one needs self-judgment under the continual refining and purifying of the LORD. Yea, rather, how one needs the refiner's fire, over and over and over again, till all the dross is purged out from the pure gold of the very word of God.

Because Mark is the shortest of the gospels, there is a tendency to suppose that it is the easiest to understand. Nothing could be further from the truth. Without doubt Mark is the most difficult of all the gospels to penetrate and to discover in its essential concept or vision of Christ.

Certainly, the central concept of Mark does not at all present Christ as the Servant. But that is not to say that the evangelist *never* refers to Christ in this way, nor that the service of God appears *nowhere* in this gospel. On the contrary, in a certain measure, both truths are apparent.

But so is a target apparent to a distant archer who can do no more than make out a circular shape at great range. Much nearer, distinct multicoloured rings appear, each concentrically ordered about the golden bull's-eye.

The Concept of Mark

That central *bull's-eye* is the mark: not merely the target. The target is not the mark: the bull's-eye is the mark. To hit the target, but miss the bull's-eye, is to miss the mark.

About forty years ago, and then again some fifteen years later, both over very long periods, I gave myself exclusively to seek out the mind of the Lord in Mark. I believe I hit the target, but *now* I know that I missed the bull's-eye, in the two different sets of notes separated by so many years.

Each study presumed Christ to be the Servant. But why did I presume? Because so many years ago I was too young and too ignorant to perceive the degree of influence spiritual-sounding men *still* held over me, and too self-distrusting to search out the root of the error which I sensed to be in the teaching of the earlier Brethren such as J.N. Darby and J.B. Stoney. *There* I erred.

But now, led once again, after so long a time—led, I may say, in fear and trembling—to seek out and open the truth from the gospel according to Mark, I have given myself to prayer and the reading of that gospel over and over again day after day for months, mostly on my knees, till I have felt the witness that has at last enabled me to set out the matter in order.

Only after this did I consider my labours from past years. It was during the reading of such previous studies that I discovered that both sets of notes proposed the concept of Christ as the Servant. But from deep within my spirit, having sought all over afresh, I was moved to throw a question—of but two words—in my own face over both sets of notes: 'Prove it'.

But I could not prove it. I could only disprove it. Servant? The idea *was* there; but no more than in Matthew and Luke. In fact there are considerably *more* references to both servant and service in Matthew and Luke than in Mark. If 'Servant' were the concept of Christ in the gospel according to Mark,

15

then why had Mark the *least* number of references to the servant and service out of the three synoptic gospels?

The fact that Mark has *some* reference to the servant and service is immaterial to the definition of the *essential* concept of the book. Such references are but one of many subsidiary and complementary parts making up the whole.

It is patently incorrect to magnify one part so that it eclipses the others comprising the sum, merely on the ground that such a part exists. Much more so when that magnification obscures the vital concept upon which the whole is focussed.

Besides, the general concept of servant is that of old testament servitude. A few places may have *typified* new testament sonship, but certainly any service seen in Mark is that of the Son *as opposed to* the old testament notion of the servant. So that just as one cannot reduce the whole to a part, neither can one diminish the thing typified to the type.

The most significant passages in the old testament foretelling or typifying Christ as the promised servant are to be found in the book of the prophet Isaiah. However these prophecies are couched in veiled and figurative language, requiring the most careful interpretation.

Although speaking of Christ, the prophet does so by referring to him *through* the names of 'Israel my servant, Jacob whom I have chosen', Isa. 41:8, repeated 44:1; and again, 'O Jacob, my servant; and thou, Jeshurun, whom I have chosen', Isa. 44:2; once more, 'Remember these, O Jacob and Israel; for thou art my servant', Isa. 44:21.

Each one of these passages, albeit ostensibly addressed to Jacob, Israel and Jeshurun, actually speak of Christ, though in restricted old testament terminology, agreeable to the contemporary limitations of the people.

Nevertheless observe that the prophet enlarges: 'And now, saith the LORD that formed me from the womb to be his servant, to bring Jacob again to him, Though Israel be not gathered, yet shall I be glorious in the eyes of the LORD, and my God shall be my strength.'

'And he said, It is a light thing that thou shouldest be my servant to raise up the tribes of Jacob, and to restore the preserved of Israel: I will also give thee for a light to the Gentiles, that thou mayest be my salvation unto the end of the earth', Isaiah 49:5,6.

Now, although this last passage speaks of the same servant as the earlier—and more obscure—places, here there is no ambiguity. Without doubt the reference is to Christ.

When at last the time of Isaiah's prophecy was fulfilled, ancient Simeon, who waited for the consolation of Israel, the Holy Ghost being upon him, knew by the Holy Ghost that he should not see death, till he had seen the Lord's Christ.

He came by the Spirit into the temple, and seeing the child Jesus, took him up in his arms and blessed God, saying, 'Now lettest thou thy servant depart in peace'. Next he prophesied of the infant Jesus, saying that he should be for 'A light to lighten the Gentiles, and the glory of thy people Israel', Luke 2:25-32.

Now, several centuries before this, Isaiah had foretold of the Lord's servant, 'I will also give thee'—besides being a glory to gather Israel—'for a light to the Gentiles, that thou mayest be my salvation unto the end of the earth', Isa. 49:6.

Almost the same words as Simeon. *But Simeon's words are recorded in Luke; not Mark.* There are no, repeat, no, such servant passages in Mark. Then how can *he* depict the servant?

Simeon—and his quotation from Isaiah—appears in Luke; Mark neither mentions him nor his prophecy. Then why is Luke not regarded as the gospel which depicts the servant? For it cannot be Mark, because there are *no* servant passages or quotations of this sort in Mark at all.

And it is not as if Mark does *not* quote old testament passages. He quotes or refers to *at least* sixty-three places from the old testament, and, at that, in the shortest of all the four gospels.

Mark is full of the old testament. Maybe: but he is empty of references to Christ as the servant. Of the sixty-three references in sixteen chapters, thirty-six are quotations, the rest allusions. But neither quote nor allusion once refers to the servant.

So many old testament passages in Mark? Then why no choice Isaiah 'servant' passages—let alone any other such old testament references—whether quotation or allusion?

If *the* object in Mark were to project Jesus as the servant, and his work as the service, why is Luke the only one of the evangelists to quote Isaiah's exclusive 'servant' passages, specifically prophesying of Christ as the servant in the service of God?

And, in contrast, why is Mark so deafening in his silence on the servant prophecies? Or is silence to be considered some great argument in favour of things that do not exist?

The entire fallacy is nothing but imposed tradition, going back to the beginnings of the apostasy, and therefore of the papacy, substituting its blind, dark, and ignorant superstition to cover over the truth, babbling fables about the eagle, the lion, the man, and the ox.

Ox? As one of our own poets says, 'The fault, dear Brutus, is not in our stars, but in ourselves'. And the fault in this bovine herd lies in their not sticking to mooing at the grass over a five barred gate, as opposed to belching out gas towards a heavens filled with dimensions of glory altogether beyond their brutish comprehension.

Mark the ox? If so, though changing the metaphor, observe that Moses also has somewhat to say to these schoolmen, Deuteronomy 22:10, 'Thou shalt not plow with an ox and an ass together'. And if those asses had been kept from plowing with these oxen, we had not suffered from the reverberations of their asinine braying to this day.

Then what *shall* be said of Mark? It is a fact that Mark's narrative has been divided into some six hundred and seventy-eight verses over sixteen chapters, preserving something short of two hundred and ninety words of Jesus. Mark is the shortest gospel.

The whole of Mark, save for some fifty-five verses, appears in Matthew and Luke. That is to say, Mark is almost completely incorporated in Matthew and Luke, the two other synoptic gospels.

Almost the entire substance of the gospel according to Mark appears in Matthew. Again, nearly half of Mark is to be found in Luke, who follows Mark's order, and records a greater proportion of the actual words of Mark.

Nevertheless, over and above the vast amount of Mark to be found in Matthew and Luke, both Matthew and Luke possess a great deal of material *peculiar to each of those gospels*.

Such unique passages in Matthew and Luke facilitate the understanding of those books. For example, in the case of Matthew, it is clear that the Spirit presents Jesus as the Messiah in terms of the kingdom of heaven. No other gospel has this distinctive teaching.

The same is true of Luke. Here, so great a number of distinctive passages—found nowhere else—help greatly in the understanding of the concept of Christ in Luke.

It is Mark's absence of this informative feature so prominent in Matthew and Luke that pin-points the difficulty precisely. Far from having a body of truth peculiar to the narrative of Mark, on the contrary, this gospel has very little to distinguish it from the other synoptics.

In comparison hardly anything is unique to Mark. Indeed, far from being distinguished, *almost the whole of Mark appears in Matthew and Luke in one form or another.*

Only fifty to fifty-five verses remain peculiar to Mark, not quoted in any other gospel. But how much do these fifty to fifty-five verses tell us about the distinct presentation of Christ in this gospel, as opposed to the vast body of truth peculiar to Matthew and Luke respectively?

In the fifty-five or so passages found only in Mark, two miracles and two parables are conspicuous: the miracle of the deaf and dumb man healed, Mk. 7:31-37, and the miracle of the blind man who received his sight at Bethsaida, Mk. 8:22-26.

The distinctive parables are those of the seed growing secretly, Mk. 4:26-29, and the parable of the man taking a far journey, leaving his house in the care of his servants under the watchfulness of the porter, Mk. 13:33-37.

Most notable is the singular absence of any genealogy combined with the remarkable account of the ascension. But notable or not, it is the *relative absence* of unique material, coupled with the incorporation of most of Mark into Matthew and Luke, that make this gospel so hard to define.

Why? Because Mark is so *like* the others—Matthew and Luke—and since *they* are so distinct, the definition of Mark, by any standards, becomes increasingly elusive, and the grasping at straws so tempting.

Nevertheless, one must resist temptation, one must trust in the heavenly Teacher, Christ, and one must believe that what is impossible with men, is possible with God.

There is an emphasis in Mark—peculiar to this gospel—on the immediacy of what Jesus *did*, so much so that the words 'straightway', 'anon', 'immediately', and 'forthwith' occur about forty times.

There are few long addresses. Where these occur, more often than not they are given in response to circumstances, developments, or queries. In no sense can these be compared with the great discourses of Matthew and Luke. Indeed Mark gives only one major discourse, recorded in thirty-seven verses in Chapter 13. The emphasis is on what Jesus *did* rather than on what he *said*.

Peter's address to Cornelius and his brethren accords with Mark. Beginning with the baptism of John, Peter speaks of Jesus preaching peace to the children of Israel; being anointed of God with the Holy Ghost and with power; of his going about doing good; of his healing all who were oppressed of the devil; and of God being with him.

Of these things the apostles were witness, as they were of the Jews having slain Jesus, hanging him on a tree; but God raised him the third day, and showed him openly. Of this his chosen witnesses bore testimony, for he ate and drank with them after he rose from the dead.

These were the apostles who were commanded of him to preach to the people after his ascension. Although these facts were Peter's testimony in Acts 10:34-43, nevertheless, in both letter and spirit, they constitute the kernel of Mark.

Mark is unique among the three synoptic gospels—namely, Matthew, Mark, and Luke—in opening with the words 'The beginning of the gospel of Jesus Christ, *the Son of God*'. Not least, I say, because the great emphasis of all three gospels is upon the proclamation of the ministry of Jesus Christ as *the Son of man*.

On only two other occasions in Mark the Father proclaims Jesus to be *the Son of God*. First at his baptism and last at his transfiguration: but neither of these occasions was public. Publicly, Jesus proclaimed himself to be the Son of man.

It is noticeable that twice devils—or demons—confessed him to be the Son of God—or Son of the most high God—and on both occasions they were rebuked for doing so, being commanded to silence.

Hence, although Mark opens with the words 'Son of God', it is essential to observe that these opening and introductory words were intended *for the saints*, to whom the narrative was addressed at the beginning.

The first occasion of the Father declaring him to be the Son was addressed *to the Son himself*; no one else: '*Thou art* my beloved Son.' It is not—in Mark—'*This is* my beloved Son.'

The last occasion was addressed to Peter, James, and John, in a mountain *apart*. Then, in a figure, this is a testimony to the apostolic ministry: 'This is my beloved Son: hear him.' On no public occasion was the name Son of God proclaimed: the public proclamation was that of the Son of man.

Jesus twice alludes to his divine Sonship in a parable speaking of a father—after dispatching many abused servants—sending his wellbeloved son—observe that he *was* son with his father *before* being sent—'Having yet therefore one son, his well-beloved, he sent him also last unto them, saying, They will reverence my son', Mk. 12:6.

But whatever the unmistakable allusion, in the parable Jesus does not actually say that the father referred to was his Father, nor does he categorically state that he was the son of whom the parable speaks. It is simply 'A certain man', who, having sent many servants had 'yet therefore one son'. But to whom Jesus referred was clear as crystal, hence the Jews 'knew that he had spoken the parable against them', Mk. 12:12.

Again, the high priest asks Jesus, 'Art thou the Christ, the Son of the Blessed?' Mk. 14:61. Observe, *he* asked Jesus: Jesus did not volunteer the information. Nevertheless he answers, 'I am', but immediately subjoins 'and ye shall see *the Son of man* sitting on the right hand of power, and coming in the clouds of heaven', Mk. 14:62.

Hence the consistency of the proclamation *in public* of Jesus as the Son of man is not broken by this passage. Nor by the last: The centurion, beholding the death of Jesus, said, 'Truly this man was the Son of God', Mark 15:39. But this was his own conclusion, not a divine revelation.

Coming now to the title *Son of man*, Matthew refers to Jesus in this way thirty-two times, Mark fourteen, and Luke on twenty-six occasions. Here one must bear in mind the comparative length of these gospels.

Son of man is a title virtually exclusive to Jesus' ministry on earth—that is, to the Jews—and to his coming again at the Last Judgment, for, testifies Peter, Acts 10:42, 'It is he which was ordained of God to be the Judge of quick and dead.'

Of the days of his flesh Jesus declares, 'I am not sent but unto the lost sheep of the house of Israel'. Then as *Son of man*, for that was the designation of the ministry in which he was sent to Israel.

The ministry of Jesus as Son of man, whilst everything to do with the Jews in the days of his flesh, was, and is—as a ministry—nothing to do with the *ecclesia*, or 'church'.

Nor—as a ministry—has the title Son of man anything to do with the revelation of the Son of God from the heavenly glory by the gospel during this present dispensation, that is, the period commencing with the day of Pentecost and concluding with the Last Day at the end of the age.

Mark records that the Son of man had power on earth to forgive sins; was Lord of the sabbath; came not to be ministered unto but to minister; and to give his life a ransom for many.

This gospel continues to inform the saints—for the book is theirs: it was never intended to be bandied about for sale in the world by traders out of steeple-houses or in the market-place—that the Son of man went as it was written of him.

He would be betrayed into the hands of sinners; he must suffer many things; must be rejected of the elders, chief priests, and scribes; must be killed; and the third day rise again.

As with Matthew, Mark passes from the texts which speak of the ministry, betrayal, rejection, and death of the Son of man at the hands of the Jewish nation, and of God raising him from the dead on the third day, immediately to his coming again in power and glory at the Last Day.

Mark does not mention the assembly, or *ecclesia*, taking the place of Israel in the counsels of God. In Mark there is no mention of the *ecclesia*—or 'church'—at all.

Nor is there anything but the rarest hint of an age-long dispensation which should come in between the ascension of Christ and his return.

From the ministry of the Son of man recorded in Mark no one could tell of the coming revelation of the hidden mystery, or of the descent of the Holy Ghost to bring in and form the *ecclesia*, or of the calling out of a people from among the

Gentiles to answer to this glorious revelation of the Son of God from heaven in the gospel.

After the rejection of the Son of man by the Jewish nation, Mark's record passes to the prophecy of his coming again. That is—so it appears—immediately from that generation to the Last Judgment. 'Whosoever therefore shall be ashamed of me and of my words in this adulterous and sinful generation; of him also shall the Son of man be ashamed, when he cometh in the glory of his Father with the holy angels.'

But between the ascension of the Son of man, and his coming again with power and great glory, there was to appear a hidden mystery. After his ascension, following the descent of the Holy Ghost, the *declaration and revelation of the Son of God*—then a hidden mystery — was to be made known from the heavenly glory, by the preaching of the gospel with apostolic authority and power.

This was the revelation of the mystery. And to those who received it, united in one, Mark addressed and addresses 'The *beginning* of the gospel of Jesus Christ, the Son of God', Mk. 1:1.

However, given these things, whilst clarifying the way in which Jesus is presented in the three synoptic gospels—and therefore Mark—this still does not answer the question, What is the concept of the second gospel?

How, and with what emphasis, is Christ presented in Mark? Applied in turn to all the evangelists, here this question is the hardest to answer. Not least because of the fact that Mark is virtually incorporated into two other gospels, making his own distinctiveness the harder to determine, because by this fact the narrative is in a manner already submerged.

It has been stressed that Matthew and Luke not only absorb Mark, but each has its own unique matter, and at considerable length, and this distinctive material, in and of itself, gives numerous pointers to the particular presentation of Christ in Matthew and Luke.

To the contrary, Mark possesses little more than fifty to fifty-five verses unique to this gospel. And out of these passages—despite the fact that two miracles and two parables are not found elsewhere—there appears little if anything to give indication of the concept of Mark.

Certainly the notion of servant must be ruled out, no matter that such a view appears here and there: the same random appearance is true of both Matthew and Luke to a demonstrably greater degree.

Servant? but from the outset Mark stresses that he is *the Son*, as opposed to a servant. Of all the synoptic gospels therefore, the second is the most emphatic. Mark opens uniquely: 'The beginning of the gospel of Jesus Christ, the *Son* of God.'

In Mark the Son of God comes forth from the Father. Throughout the narrative he fulfils the work which he was sent to accomplish, in a way peculiarly emphasized by this gospel. At the conclusion, having accomplished that work, he returns to the Father.

This is corroborated by the parable, 'Last of all he sent his son'. But what did the son do? He called to account the stewards of his father's vineyard, to yield up the fruits thereof. However, the worthless character of those husbandmen had been foreshadowed by their murderous treatment of the many who had been sent prior to the coming of the son.

The old covenant had *failed*. In a word, Israel, and man in Israel, was already a *proven failure*, for, as to God's servants the prophets, in turn they were beaten, sent empty away, stoned, wounded, killed or otherwise condemned.

But 'Having yet therefore one son, his wellbeloved, he sent him also last unto them, saying, They will reverence my son.' But they did not reverence his son. They said, 'This is the heir; come, let us kill him, and the inheritance shall be ours.'

And as they said, so they did. But shall the inheritance be theirs? Hear the Son: 'What shall therefore the lord of the vineyard do? he will come and destroy the husbandmen, and will give the vineyard unto others.'

Now note Jesus' conclusion: 'And have ye not read this scripture; The stone which the builders rejected is become the head of the corner: this was the Lord's doing, and it is marvellous in our eyes?'

Now, *that* points to the concept of Mark. But one never finds anything more explicit than such veiled pointers. As men would call it, Straws in the wind. But since those straws are borne in but one direction, then by this movement the invisible wind—which bloweth where it listeth—may be discerned.

It is from such consistent suggestions and allusions that the drift of Mark will be perceived, and, if so, the concept itself discovered. From no more than the parable, it is apparent that the Son came forth from the Father into a scene in which malicious—and indeed murderous—priests and scribes had long since stolen the things of God established at the beginning.

These are the 'husbandmen' of God's vineyard, who, generation by generation, rejected and slew countless prophets and wise men sent to them. These held the common people in bondage to an old covenant hopelessly broken in the uncircumcision of their hearts, and rendered unrecognizable by the imposition of traditions invented by them and their fathers in place of God's commandments.

It was not as if all this were not foreknown, nor that the depravity of men in religion was not perceived to be incorrigible.

27

However, God would bring everything under the full exposure of the light from heaven by the presence of his own Son, so that 'those wicked husbandmen' would be without excuse.

But for all that—and the necessity of it—this exposure was not the moving cause of the coming of the Son. Rather it was the effect. But the moving cause of his glorious appearing stood in a hidden mystery that was yet to be revealed.

The old testament, the whole covenant in principle, had achieved nothing save the overwhelming evidence of ineradicable and inbred sin; Israel had revolted; the entire old system of religion had proved itself ineffectual; the Jews had become alienated beyond remedy.

Nevertheless the Father sent the Son, he came into the world, he was made manifest to Israel, beginning with the baptism of John. This was 'The beginning of the gospel of Jesus Christ, the Son of God', Mk. 1:1. Then, despite the abounding of sin, grace much more abounded, and a new beginning, a dawning era, began to shine in the new testament.

There is nothing *apparently* peculiar or unique to the gospel according to Mark. It is the uniqueness of his person, his peerless works, his appalling rejection, and, beyond all, his breathtaking vindication that are most conspicuous. It is *himself*, his witness in the gospel, that is so striking.

Negatively, it is true, Mark shows the destruction of the wicked husbandmen, the end of the old covenant, the judgment of Israel. But infinitely more is revealed. Positively, here is the new testament, the beginning of the gospel, the heralding of the reign of the Son of God from the glory of heaven.

Mark conceives a new thing. To this end he postulates the mediator of the new testament. He predicates the apostle of the new covenant. This is the dawning of the day. It is the witness of Jesus. By definition, Mark testifies to 'The *beginning* of the gospel of Jesus Christ, the Son of God', Mk. 1:1.

Mark is a gospel that appears to emphasize the dynamic energy of the person and work of Christ, rather than his doctrine and insight: but appearances are deceptive. In fact a profound concept awaits the patient seeker after the essence of the truth in Mark.

The vigour and power of the forceful narrative make it immediately obvious that *the Son* is being marked out. And yet such dynamic narration is not the whole, neither is it the profoundest depth of this gospel.

There is a concept beyond the obvious that definitively distinguishes Jesus Christ in the gospel according to Mark. To perceive this, an inner patience and discernment must carefully trace the breathings of the Spirit almost imperceptibly sustained throughout the narrative.

Heedlessly to accept the traditional notion of 'Servant' is to miss the gentle accumulation of hints, allusions, insinuations and nuances, found throughout this gospel.

Servant? It is just what the concept of Christ in Mark is not. As opposed to a servant, he is the Son. A servant is no heir. The Son is the heir. That is why the servants or husbandmen said, 'This is the heir; come, let us kill him, and the inheritance shall be ours.' But the Son, risen from the dead, though once rejected of those builders, is now become head of the corner.

If so, there is a new building in view, new sonship in prospect, and, of necessity, a new covenant in effect. In that he saith, A new covenant, he hath made the first old. Now that which decayeth and waxeth old is ready to vanish away. But a new, a divine, an everlasting covenant cannot decay, it will never wax old, neither can it ever vanish away.

This is precisely what the Son has established in the resurrection. And both the prophet and Mark concur, as the Son himself quotes: 'This was the Lord's doing, and it is marvellous in our eyes.' Here we touch the concept of Mark.

A thing easily missed—for the obvious *is* easily missed—waits to be discovered in the unique opening and closing of the gospel according to Mark.

In both Matthew and Luke there are genealogies, though tracing different lines. But there is no genealogy at all in Mark: no birth; no childhood: nothing. Nothing but an abrupt entry, nothing other than a bursting forth from eternity into time, from deity into humanity.

Particularly, there is no ascension in Matthew. There is a reason, and this has been expounded in the concise work which I have delivered on that gospel. To the contrary, in Luke there is an ascension, but this differs in numerous points from that in Mark. In Mark it is more abrupt, more conclusive; it is the final word: 'He was received up into heaven', Mk. 16:19.

Between his coming into the world and his being received up out of it, there is such supernatural vitality, such divine energy, such extraordinary testimony, such heavenly witness.

Even the pace of the narrative—'immediately'; 'straightway'—conveys such freshness, so much spiritual vigour. He is being *marked out*. It is not simply *what* he says, *what* he does — astounding as that is—it is the *he* who is saying it, and it is his *way* of doing it, that is distinguished. It is *his uniqueness* that Mark emphasizes.

This finds a parallel in Hebrews 1:1,2, 'God, who at sundry times and in divers manners spake in time past unto the fathers by the prophets, hath in these last days spoken unto us in Son.' For the Greek reads literally '*in* Son'. Now *that* is Mark. It is *the speaker*, before the speech begins. Indeed his person *is* the speech.

It is not 'spoken unto us *by* the Son.' That would be his utterance. It is spoken unto us 'in Son'. Before he opens his mouth to speak, attention is drawn to the truth that by virtue of the coming of his unique person, God has *already* spoken.

The speaker, properly, embodies the speech. When *he* is considered, already there exists peerless speech: it is the last word. Indeed, it is speech without words, so breathtaking is the person of the speaker. No matter what may be voiced or done by him thereafter, his very existence utters volumes. That is precisely the concept in which Hebrews and Mark agree.

Of course it is, because there is such an analogy between the concept of Mark, and the development of Hebrews. Take Mark: Is there no beginning to the humanity of Jesus? Does the Son of God simply *appear* in manhood? After the ascension, is there no end to Jesus' humanity? Does he simply *disappear*, 'received up into heaven'?

Consider these questions in terms of the epistle to the Hebrews. Specifically the writer speaks of Jesus Christ the Son of God *by interpretation* from Melchisedec saying: 'Without father, without mother, without descent, having neither beginning of days, nor end of life; but made like unto the Son of God; abideth a priest continually', Heb. 7:3.

But this is precisely Mark's concept. To indicate that concept, Mark leaves out the genealogy; he omits reference to Mary; nothing appears of Jesus' birth. He is made manifest as if he had—in his manhood—no beginning of days.

Christ disappears, risen and received up into heaven, because he has—in his manhood—no end of life. However, since that manhood *is* the humanity of the Son of God, he is not—as was Melchisedec—made '*like unto*' the Son of God: he *is* the Son of God. 'The beginning of the gospel of Jesus Christ, the Son of God', Mk. 1:1.

By the Holy Ghost, Mark is inspired to fashion his narrative to convey this concept. Is God about to give words and deeds by his Son? Then, commands the opening narrative, *Consider* the Son, before he speaks. Consider the Speaker. Consider the Apostle and High Priest of our profession. Consider 'The beginning of the gospel of Jesus Christ, the Son of God.'

'In Son.' It is he who is being marked out. The patriarchs, Abraham, Moses, David, the prophets, none was like unto 'Jesus Christ, the Son of God'. How could they be? Peerless, unique, divine, he is the second man, the last Adam, and, from the beginning of the gospel, this was obvious beyond the least shadow of doubt.

Servant? But he is the Son. What servant can answer to that everlasting divine relationship? And is he manifest in human nature? Then he is no servant, but a new man, a second man, a life-giving spirit, the last Adam. The term servant, however prophetically used or typically depicted, could never rise to this matchless concept of divine sonship.

But this is how Mark opens his gospel: not 'made like unto' the Son of God, but the Son of God himself: 'The beginning of the gospel of Jesus Christ, the Son of God', Mk. 1:1. Then Mark does not, and cannot, depict Christ as servant. It is not at all the concept of the book. Mark's concept of Christ is vastly greater: it is literally immense.

Servant? But it is just this notion which Mark *avoids* in his awesome and magnificent portrayal of Christ.

Moses was 'a servant in the house', yes: 'But Christ as a Son over his own house', Heb. 3:6. And, saith Jesus in John, 'The servant abideth not in the house for ever: but the Son abideth ever', John 8:35.

Hebrews 3:1 exhorts, 'Wherefore, holy brethren, partakers of the heavenly calling, consider the Apostle and High Priest of our profession, Christ Jesus.' But where are we to consider him in such offices? In the new testament. These are offices essential to the bringing in of a new covenant.

Hebrews states that such offices in Christ are 'of our profession', as opposed to Israel's profession. The profession of Israel was that of the old covenant. It was mediated through angels, spoken by Moses, and administered in Aaron. These were, respectively, the mediator, the apostle, and the high priest of *their*—old testament—profession.

But the holy brethren, partakers of the heavenly calling, are not of that profession. They profess the new testament, of which the Son of God is at once the mediator, the apostle, and the high priest in his own singular person.

As mediator he was sent from God to man in his eternal and divine Sonship. As priest he answered for man to God in the perfection of his impeccable humanity. As apostle Jesus Christ brought in and speaks forth the new and everlasting covenant declared in and by his own person.

Risen from the dead, ascended to the right hand of God, ministering from the heavenly glory, on the ground of one sacrifice offered once for all, 'He abideth a priest continually'. He ever lives to make intercession for all those for whom he had wrought eternal redemption through his blood.

Therefore the consideration of the High Priest of our profession is preceded by the fact of his sacrificial death, the consequence of his glorious resurrection, and follows upon his ascension into heaven to sit upon God's right hand in the everlasting glory.

Thence he exercises his High Priesthood, 'Called a priest for ever after the order of Melchisedec.' Clearly, apart from the actual record of the ascension, the exposition of this glorious priesthood lies beyond the scope of Mark, 'The *beginning* of the gospel of Jesus Christ, the Son of God'.

Mark neither professes nor intends to convey the continuance, the end, or the fulness of that gospel which it is his stated purpose to set forth at its beginning.

But that beginning must include—it demands—the bringing down of the new covenant from God out of heaven by the Son as mediator. The beginning of the gospel positively requires the assertion of the truth that *the Son* was manifest in the flesh. It necessitates the concept of the Son's apostleship, being the speaker of, and consequently speaking forth that covenant which he had brought into the world in his own person.

These are things well within the scope of the gospel according to Mark. More. These are things that are of the *essence* in Mark. Because they are, in and of themselves, 'The *beginning* of the gospel of Jesus Christ, the Son of God', Mark 1:1.

'For if that first covenant had been faultless, then should no place have been sought for the second', Heb. 8:7. But if a second, then a new.

And if a new, then an everlasting covenant, founded upon better promises, having a better mediatorship than that of angels — who could neither ascend to God nor descend to man—and a better apostle, who is God's speech 'in Son'.

Moreover, this covenant is established on a sacrifice better than all that preceded, namely, one sacrifice for sins for ever, being administered by an everlasting priesthood, as it is said, 'Thou art a priest for ever after the order of Melchisedec'.

Now this truth so wonderfully set forth in Hebrews encompasses the whole of the gospel. But if so, of necessity, that whole incorporates *the beginning*. And of that *beginning* it is written, 'The beginning of the gospel of Jesus Christ, the Son of God'.

Mark opens by declaring abruptly the Son who came from God into the world. 'Wherefore when he cometh into the world, he saith, Sacrifice and offering thou wouldest not, but a body hast thou prepared me.' 'Then said he, Lo, I come to do thy will, O God. He taketh away the first, that he may establish the second', Heb. 10:5,9.

Now, his coming into the world to do the will of God in the body prepared for him, his taking away the first covenant to establish the second, in a word, his apostleship, together with his sacrificial death, his glorious resurrection, and his being received up into heaven, are things not merely recorded in Mark: they are of the very essence to the peerless concept of Christ presented in this gospel.

In all the vast range of truth incorporated in the beginning of the gospel of Jesus Christ, the Son of God, the thing that is *central*, the thing that is of the essence, the concept itself, stands in Mark's delineation of *the apostle of the new testament*.

Here—in a figure unique among the four gospels—Jesus Christ appears without father, without mother, without genealogy, without beginning of days, or end of years, the Son of God, come down from and received up into heaven to abide continually, a priest for ever after the order of Melchisedec.

Hence the gospel according to Mark closes—at the end of the beginning—with his being seated at the right hand of God, thence to administer the new covenant from the heavenly glory.

But first—possessed of such origins, and having such destiny—the Son is sent forth from God to mediate and to bring in the new testament. At once he is marked out in his peerless humanity — 'in Son' — showing throughout the narrative of

Mark, and in the order of events, the anointing and seal of
the Father resting upon his unique apostleship.

But nothing is obvious. Everything is spiritual. And if spiritual, the indications are restrained, the leading is gentle, and
the interior reality is hidden beneath the outward appearance.

But it is there: it is not so hidden that it is not revealed to
those that wait upon the Lord, who are brought into the secret.
It is there: there in the abruptness of Christ's appearance at the
baptism of John. And there in the swiftness of his disappearance
into heaven at the ascension.

It is there: there in the dynamic life and vitality that surges
through every verse, every paragraph, every chapter, constant
in the narrative: 'In Son'.

The speaker of the covenant, God's speaker, is being made
manifest; it is he *himself*, not only his deeds and words, *his
person* to which attention is drawn.

It is there: his divine and supernatural vigour vibrates
throughout the narrative: 'In the beauties of holiness from
the womb of the morning: thou hast the dew of thy youth.'

It is there: sometimes in but one word hidden in a parable.
'Having yet therefore one son, he sent'—the Greek is *apostellō*
—'he *sent* him also last unto them', Mk. 12:6. *Apostellō*, yes,
but the English noun form is *Apostle*. The Apostle of the new
testament: the Son. *There* is the concept of Mark.

It is there: concealed, perhaps, in the translation of Mark
9:37, 'Whosoever shall receive me, receiveth not me, but him
that sent'—once more the Greek is *apostellō*—'that *sent* me.'
Sent *me*. Then, as the apostle of the new testament.

It is there: even when no more than implied in the use of the word *apostellō* in the case of John the Baptist at the very beginning of the gospel: 'Behold, I send'—*apostellō*—'send my messenger before thy face', Mk. 1:2. And if his *herald* be as his old covenant apostle, then what kind of apostle is he himself, who both mediates and speaks the new covenant?

It is there in *his* sending his *own* apostles—Mk. 6:30 'And the apostles gathered themselves together unto Jesus'—to preach the kingdom of God, for 'The time is fulfilled'.

What time is fulfilled, or concluded? Why, the time of the old covenant, and the waiting for Christ to bring in the new: that is fulfilled. 'And the kingdom of God is at hand: repent ye, and believe the *gospel*', Mk. 1:15. Now everybody knows, the gospel is that of the new testament of our Lord and Saviour Jesus Christ.

It is there in the Apostle of our profession ordaining his apostles: Mk. 3:14, 'He ordained twelve, that they should be with him, and that he might send'—the Greek is *apostellō*—'*send* them forth to preach.'

Again, Mk. 6:7, 'And he called unto him the twelve, and began to send them forth'—*apostellō*—'to *send* them forth by two and two.'

And it is there in the last word: 'Then shall he send'—*apostellō* —'he shall *send* his angels, and shall gather together his elect from the four winds, from the uttermost part of the earth to the uttermost part of heaven.' If that is not apostolic, What is?

It is there in the comparison of Moses—the apostle of the old covenant, Israel's profession—with that of the apostle of our— new covenant—profession, Heb. 3:1. Indisputably, in such a context, *the apostle speaks forth the covenant*. And in this context, there being two covenants respectively, there can be but two apostles in relation to their speech.

And is it credible, think you, that out of the four gospels, *not one* should set forth the central concept of Christ in terms of his paramount significance as *the apostle of the new testament*, without which and save for whom we would abide in darkness, blind to the knowledge of the covenant, and oblivious of the truth of the one mediator between God and man?

For, although many passages in Mark are duplicated in the other, larger, gospels, we know by the material unique to *them* that *they* have a special overriding vision of Christ to present.

Whence it follows that to *Mark*, with his short, graphic, vivid presentation, belongs the distinctive arrangement of his own unique verses, together with many passages common to all the synoptic gospels—Matthew, Mark, and Luke—peculiarly to honour the Son of God as the apostle of the new testament.

For instance, under Moses the people received manna from heaven as bread to eat. But 'Moses gave you not that bread from heaven'. No, the LORD gave it, though under Moses' apostleship. Then what kind of apostle is he who gave from his own hands on earth bread multiplied beyond measure from a few loaves first to five thousand then to four thousand? Answer, the apostle of the *new* covenant.

Again, Moses led Israel through the waters. But who parted the Red Sea? Not Moses, but the Son from heaven, there called, the LORD. And did Moses, under whom the LORD parted the waters, ever *walk* on the water? No, but our apostle did.

Once more, Moses gave the fiery law, and the angels mediated it, in the midst of the tempest, when the mountains shook and the earth trembled. But the Son of God—'Let all the angels of God worship him'—*stilled* the tempest, *calmed* the raging waves, and said to both the wind and the sea, Peace; be still. And it was so. This is the word of our apostle.

Above all, Mark shows the astounding *newness* of the gospel of Jesus Christ, the Son of God, from its beginning. This appears over and again in the apostolic ministry of Christ: 'And they were astonished at his doctrine: for he taught them as one that had *authority*, and *not* as the scribes', Mk. 1:22.

Again, 'And they were all amazed, insomuch that they questioned among themselves, saying, What thing is this? what *new* doctrine is this? for with *authority* commandeth he even the unclean spirits, and *they do obey him*', Mk. 1:27.

Once more, 'They were all amazed, and glorified God, saying, We never saw it on this fashion', Mk. 2:12. It is a *new* fashion. Take that Greek word, *kainos*—new, fresh, newly made—'This is my blood of the *new* testament', Mk. 14:24. 'They shall speak with *new* tongues', Mk. 16:17. It is Mark that stresses such apostolic truth.

Or take the parable of new cloth sewn on an old garment; or new wine put into old bottles: 'No man seweth a piece of new'— *agnaphos*, unsmoothed, unfinished —'cloth on an old garment: else the new'—*kainos*, fresh, newly made—'piece that filled it up taketh away from the old, and the rent is made worse.' This is the very concept of Mark, despite that the *incident* may be found elsewhere in the synoptic gospels.

'And no man putteth new'—*neos*, new, young—'wine into old bottles: else the new'—*neos*—'wine doth burst the bottles, and the wine is spilled, and the bottles will be marred: but new'—*neos*—'wine must be put into new'—*kainos*, new, fresh, newly made—'bottles', Mk. 2:21,22.

Mark in particular shows that this precisely illustrates the case with the old testament and those who received the old words of its past apostle, as opposed to those who receive the new words of the present apostle of the new testament. For it is certain, the Father has retained the best robe, and kept the best wine, till last.

This newness appears also in the scripture 'The stone which the builders rejected is become the head of the corner', Mk. 12:10.

The builders are those who failed under the old covenant. The stone which they rejected is the Son of God. The head of the corner is the stone from which an entirely new and wholly divine building takes both its substance and its rise.

So saith Peter, 'To whom coming, as unto a living stone, disallowed indeed of men, but chosen of God, and precious, ye also, as lively stones, are built up a spiritual house', I Pet. 2:4,5. This is apostolic building.

Peter continues, 'Wherefore also it is contained in the scripture, Behold, I lay in Sion a chief corner stone, elect, precious: and he that believeth on him shall not be confounded. Unto you therefore which believe he is precious: but unto them which be disobedient, the stone which the builders disallowed, the same is made the head of the corner', I Pet. 2:6,7.

With this Paul concurs, speaking of those called out from among the Gentiles as 'Fellowcitizens with the saints, and of the household of God, built upon the foundation of the apostles and prophets, Jesus Christ himself being the chief corner stone; in whom all the building fitly framed together groweth unto an holy temple in the Lord: in whom ye also are builded together for an habitation of God through the Spirit', Eph. 2:19-22.

This is the result of the apostolic doctrine of the new testament being administered from the glory in heaven. But it all began in Israel on earth at 'The beginning of the gospel of Jesus Christ, the Son of God', Mk. 1:1. And if at the beginning, then mediatorially and apostolically promulgated.

But of the time under the old testament, the apostle of the new speaks clearly, saying to its builders and custodians, 'Well hath Esaias prophesied of you hypocrites, as it is written, This people honoureth me with their lips, but their heart is far from me. Howbeit in vain do they worship me, teaching for doctrines the commandments of men', Mk. 7:6,7.

Wherefore the apostle of our profession finds fault with them, saying, 'If that first covenant had been faultless, then should no place have been sought for the second', Heb. 8:7. 'Then said he, Lo, I come to do thy will, O God. He *taketh away the first*'—wherefore?—'that he may establish the second.' And how otherwise, than as its apostle?

So Mark goes on to record the apostolic declaration of the new testament: 'Do ye not perceive, that whatsoever thing from without entereth into the man, it cannot defile him; *because it entereth not into his heart*, but into the belly, and goeth out into the draught.'

'And he said, That which *cometh out* of the man, *that* defileth the man. For *from within, out of the heart of men*, proceed evil thoughts, adulteries, fornications, murders, thefts, covetousness, wickedness, deceit, lasciviousness, an evil eye, blasphemy, pride, foolishness: all these evil things *come from within*, and defile the man', Mk. 7:18-23.

If so, the old covenant, and the law given by Moses, being in the letter and form of outward commandments, could not and cannot in their nature so much as reach to the heart, much less change it, or subdue the interior depravity of man.

Hence, God found fault with that old covenant, yea, with the entire legal system, and took away the first, because it was weak through the flesh, and could not touch the root, namely, the depraved heart of man. But the apostle of the new covenant, which he spake forth with such authority, could do all that which the first could not. Hence, 'He taketh away the first, that he may establish the second.'

Of this the prophets bear witness: 'Then'—in the days of the new covenant—'will I sprinkle clean water upon you, and ye shall be clean: from all your filthiness, and from all your idols, will I cleanse you.'

'A new heart also will I give you, and a new spirit will I put within you: and I will take away the stony heart out of your flesh, and I will give you an heart of flesh.'

'And I will put my spirit within you, and cause you to walk in my statutes, and ye shall keep my judgments, and do them', Ezek. 36:25-27.

So saith the prophet Isaiah: 'For thus saith the high and lofty One that inhabiteth eternity, whose name is Holy; I dwell in the high and holy place, with him also that is of a contrite and humble spirit, to revive the spirit of the humble, and to revive the heart of the contrite ones', Isa. 57:15.

And again, 'But to this man will I look, even to him that is poor and of a contrite spirit, and trembleth at my word', Isa. 66:2.

David says the same: 'Behold, I was shapen in iniquity; and in sin did my mother conceive me. Behold, thou desirest truth in the inward parts: and in the hidden part thou shalt make me to know wisdom.'

'Create in me a clean heart, O God; and renew a right spirit within me. Cast me not away from thy presence; and take not thy holy spirit from me', Psa. 51:5-6, 10-11.

Now, this is pleading for the ministry of the new testament—David having been mortified under the failure of the old—and agrees precisely with the testimony of the Son in Mk. 7:18-23. For David could not abide the state of his heart under that old, legal testament. Hence his pleading with God in Psalm 51.

Now, this was looking for and coming to Christ in the promise of the new testament with a witness.

And this the apostle of our profession confirms, saying, 'For if that first covenant had been faultless, then should no place have been sought for the second.' 'For this is the covenant that I will make with the house of Israel after those days, saith the Lord; I will put my laws *into their mind*, and write them *in their hearts*', Heb. 8:7,10.

This is the ministry of the apostle of the new testament, the ability of whom to bring in the covenant appears so wonderfully on earth in 'The *beginning* of the gospel of Jesus Christ, the Son of God', Mk. 1:1.

Risen, glorified, ascended, received into heaven, the fulness of the administration of the new testament commenced through the ministry of 'Him that speaketh from heaven', Heb. 12:25.

He speaks through his chosen witness on earth, able ministers of the new testament, effectual in their calling: 'Ye are manifestly declared to be the epistle of Christ ministered by us, written not with ink, but with the Spirit of the living God; not in tables of stone, but in fleshy tables of the heart', II Cor. 3:3. This brings in by Jesus Christ from the heavenly glory, that which he began to speak on earth, Mk. 1:1.

It is there — the concept of Christ's *apostleship of the new testament* is there—there in the faintest of impressions; there in the spiritual suggestiveness; there in the barely perceptible indications; there hidden beneath the obvious in the gospel according to Mark, 'The beginning of the gospel of Jesus Christ, the Son of God'.

If Son, then apostle. Hebrews 3:1,exhorting the holy brethren to consider the apostle of our profession, informs them in what particular: 'This man was counted worthy of more glory than Moses, inasmuch as he who hath builded the house hath more honour than the house', Heb. 3:3.

To consider the apostle of our profession, therefore, we must consider 'Christ as a Son over his own house', Heb. 3:6. If so, since Mark is concerned to depict Christ in his apostolic office, then of necessity—as Hebrews 3:6 proposes—the building of the house of God must be in view. See Mark 12:10,11.

Or rather, *the house* will be alluded to, for at this stage, in the beginning, it is a question of the apostle laying the foundations.

But certainly the spiritual indications and divine intimations of the apostolic building of the house of God will be apparent from time to time beneath the surface of the text, to be discovered by the spiritually discerning.

Take, for example, Mk. 2:1, the raising up of the man sick of the palsy. Now, Matthew tells us that this incident took place 'In his own city', Mt. 9:1.

The concept of the 'city' is peculiar to the son of David, the Messiah, and agrees with the scope of Matthew's presentation of Christ. Indeed, Matthew speaks of 'the city of the great King'.

The administration of the kingdom by a greater than David, from a heavenly Jerusalem above all, appears as the visionary and spiritual revelation distinctive of that gospel which has the Messiah and the kingdom of heaven as its concept.

Luke, however, contrasts the Pharisees and doctors of the law — with their legal presumption and forensic hauteur — helpless before Jesus 'as he was teaching', the sick laid before him, 'and the power of the Lord was present to heal them'.

In such a contrast, to the impotent rage of the powerless hierarchy whose words brought nothing but confusion, bondage, and despair, the sick of the palsy was healed by the word of Jesus, Lk. 5:16-26. Here is a contrasting ministry.

But Mark does not present the Messiah and the kingdom, nor, therefore, the city. Nor is it his purpose to contrast the power of the Lord in his word with the impotence of the legalists in the dead letter, confronted by the helplessness of the palsied man.

I say, Mark is different. Unique. In Mark the sick of the palsy was healed not 'in the city'—Matthew—nor with 'Pharisees and doctors of the law sitting'—Luke—but, Mark 2:1, 'In *the house*'.

Another passage—one peculiar to Mark—points in the same direction. 'And all the city was gathered together at the door', Mk. 1:33. But 'the door' pertains to the house. Likewise consider Mark 2:26, a place in which David is said to go *into* 'the house of God'.

Once more, notice that Mk. 3:13-19 narrates the ordination of the twelve; their being taught and empowered; their being named each one; and then, *immediately*, Mk. 3:19, 'they went into an house'. This passage also is unique to Mark.

Mk. 7:17 informs us, 'When he was entered into the house from the people, his disciples asked him concerning the parable.' By 'the house' we are pointed to 'the house of God, which is the ecclesia of the living God, the pillar and ground of the truth', I Tim. 3:15. In *this* house, the apostle opens the truth by revelation to the holy brethren, separated from 'the people'.

Once more, Mk. 7:24, Jesus having come into the borders of Tyre and Sidon, 'entered into an house'. The passage intimates that access is available into the house for the poor and oppressed from among the Gentiles. This reference also is unique to Mark.

Yet another place is characteristic of the allusions in Mark to the house of God, and the liberty of the children of God to enter, separated from the world, 'And when he was come into the house, *his disciples asked him privately*', Mk. 9:28. Similarly Mk. 9:33 shows their intimate familiarity in the house: 'And being in the house *he* asked *them*', that is, his own disciples.

Furthermore in another text it is recorded that 'In the house his disciples asked him again of the same matter', Mk. 10:10. This reference is peculiar to Mark.

Likewise the following place is exclusive to the second gospel: 'He would not suffer that any man should carry any vessel through the temple', Mk. 11:16. Why not? Because the temple was *his* house, not *their* convenience, as it is written, Mk. 11:17, 'My house shall be called of all nations *the house* of prayer.'

Passage after passage occurs in which the figurative—or even mystical—reference to 'the house' alludes to the house of God in 'The beginning of the gospel of Jesus Christ, the Son of God', Mk. 1:1.

Here appears abundant spiritual evidence to all with eyes to see, ears to hear, and a heart to understand, that such quotations as these point to 'Christ as a Son over his own house', and, if so, then as the apostle of our profession.

And not only passage after passage. Again and again the references are exclusive to Mark, giving clear indication of the spiritual concept of the gospel according to Mark.

Take one of the two parables unique to this gospel. What could be clearer? Above all from material peculiar to Mark? 'For the Son of man is as a man taking a far journey, who left *his house*, and gave authority to his servants, and to every man his work, and commanded the porter to watch.'

'Watch ye therefore: for ye know not when *the master of the house* cometh, at even, or at midnight, or at the cockcrowing, or in the morning: lest coming suddenly he find you sleeping.

And what I say unto you I say unto all, Watch', Mk. 13:34-37. Here the apostle of our profession, ascended on high as Son over the house, gives authority and commandment to his servants, to every man, and to the porter, respectively.

And this word, following from the foundation truth of the house, I Tim. 3:15, extends to all: 'What I say unto you I say unto *all.*'

As to that foundation truth—so needful to be recovered today, and reiterated by him that speaketh from heaven— where shall such vital doctrine be more clearly expressed than in the commencement of the speech of the apostle of our profession, namely, 'The beginning of the gospel of Jesus Christ, the Son of God', Mk. 1:1?

Instances might be multiplied from the gospel according to Mark either demonstrating the apostleship of Christ in bringing in the new testament, or in manifesting the things indissolubly bound to his appearing and purpose in that divine office. Multiplied yes: but none of these is obvious: everything is spiritual: nothing is superficially apparent.

These are truths that must be revealed. They are there, but they are mysteriously hidden by the Spirit from the wise and prudent, Mt. 11:25. These are spiritual things, foolishness to the natural man, I Cor. 2:13,14.

These are things awaiting the discovery of the spiritual, who, being enabled by that same Spirit to penetrate beneath the external description, enter into the essence of the gospel by revelation: 'For the Spirit searcheth all things, yea, the deep things of God', I Cor. 2:9,10.

I say, instances might be multiplied. But sufficient has been shown both from the entire context of the gospel according to Mark, and from certain detail in that context, of the imperceptible insistence of the Spirit in case after case: yet all signified in a way that avoids the gaze of the curious and superficial reader, and conceals these things from the carnal wisdom of the worldly wise.

However, for all this, I will give yet one further confirmation of the concept already made apparent—I trust—to the satisfaction of the saints, and agreement of the people of God.

One of the most revealing truths peculiar to Mark appears in the vision seen by the women at the sepulchre on the day of the resurrection.

Not only does this vision differ from those recorded in the other gospels—for each writer selects by the Spirit out of many crowded events that alone which suits the doctrine of his particular narrative — but it is of immense significance in revealing the concept of Mark.

More: Mark sets forth the vision at the tomb both in contrast with and in comparison to other places in his own gospel, so that both contrast and comparison emphasize what is being revealed.

Mk. 14:51,52—yet another passage unique to this gospel—states: 'And there followed him a certain young man, having a linen cloth cast about his naked body; and the young men laid hold on him: and he left the linen cloth, and fled from them naked.'

This incident occurred when Jesus, having been betrayed by Judas, was taken at Gethsemane. 'And they all forsook him, and fled', Mk. 14:50.

Clearly the Spirit signifies a mystery by this incident peculiar to Mark. Furthermore one must remark once again how the sheer spirituality, the gentle breathing of the hints and nuances remarkable to Mark—and so essential to the understanding of this gospel—reveal themselves only to the inward sensitiveness and interior perception of the earnest seeker after truth.

These are things brutally trampled underfoot by those who have put themselves forward as interpreters. Commentators? They are conspicuous by nothing other than being oblivious to all that is spiritual, and verbose in all that is carnal. Thus these hidden mysteries in Mark are in their case nothing more than pearls cast before swine.

In the Greek of the new testament there are four distinct words for linen. One of these, *sindōn*, occurs six times in all. Of the six, *four* of the references occur in Mark. The first time *sindōn*—fine linen; linen; or linen cloth—appears in this gospel is in the case of the young man 'who followed him'—that is, followed Jesus—'having a linen cloth'—*sindōna*—'cast about his naked body', Mk. 14:51,52.

But all his following was nothing worth in the issue, it was a loose outward cover, just like his linen cloth. The entire flimsy fabric was shed in a moment, indicative of the vanity of the form of following Christ without the substance. The young man's nakedness and destitution of inward righteousness appeared before both God and men, when, under temptation and persecution, instead of following, 'he fled naked'.

If so, all his show of righteousness was no better than filthy rags, an ephemeral inadequacy left in the hands of the enemies of Christ, making a hollow mockery of his airy and chaffy profession of following the Lord.

Yet even for some of these Christ died. 'While we were yet sinners, Christ died for us', Rom. 5:8. And again, 'When we were enemies'—then—'we were reconciled to God by the death of his Son', Rom. 5:10. Once more, 'For we ourselves'—like this young man—'were sometimes foolish, disobedient, deceived.'

But this young man was not deceived, when, fearing for his safety, he fled from Christ in the hour of temptation, leaving his rags of righteousness — his *sindōna* — in the hands of the crucifiers of the Lord of glory. 'After that' — mark it, *after that*—'the kindness and love of God our Saviour toward man appeared', Titus 3:3,4.

But how did it appear? By his carrying our iniquities; by his bearing our sins—that is, sins of self-righteousness, heinous and obnoxious in God's sight, every part as much as outwardly gross sins and iniquities—'who bare our *sins* in his own body on the tree', I Pet. 2:24.

In the case of the young man, whose *sindōna* signified the rags of self-righteousness left behind to flee from Christ under persecution, Christ took all this upon him—as it were, took the young man's worthless *sindōna* upon him—bearing it into death and the grave.

'And Pilate marvelled if he were already dead: and calling unto him the centurion, he asked him whether he had been any while dead. And when he knew it of the centurion, he gave the body to Joseph.'

'And he bought fine linen'—*sindōna*, the third reference in Mark, and the *first* after the incident of the young man—'and took him down'—that is, from the cross—'and wrapped him in the linen'—*sindōna*—'and laid him in a sepulchre', Mk. 15:44-46.

Christ *already* having borne in his own body on the tree the young man's sins of self-righteous and vain outward following—so obnoxious to the wrath of God—and having washed away every defilement and all uncleanness through his own blood, this effectual purging was signified by the clean *sindōna* in which his dead body was wrapped *after being taken down from the cross*.

In the figure, the young man's robe had been washed and made white in the blood of the Lamb—shed on the cross—of which washing the fine, clean and pure *sindōna* wrapped about the dead body of Jesus bore mute testimony.

But there is more. There is always more. One must follow from the cross to the grave. The clean *sindōna* indicated the taking away of all defilement, even from so great a sin as that of denying one's profession and fleeing from the Lord in the day of persecution and affliction.

However this cleansing was clearly made manifest immediately after the cross. That is, *before* the burial. The question remains, *After* the burial, the body being entombed, the sepulchre sealed, What appears? The answer is, *Nothing appears.*

How could anything appear? Everything—but everything—had been taken out of sight by burial. The great stone sealed the tomb. It was as if even the record had been *for ever removed from the remembrance of God and man.*

The very robe wrapped about the Saviour in death—already having been made clean through his shed blood on the cross in a figure—was itself concealed from view, entombed in the sepulchre by his burial. In another figure, 'Buried with him by baptism into death', Rom. 6:4.

So effective was the atonement, and so efficacious the blood of Christ, that no more graphic a sign could exist to portray the finality of the work of Christ: 'For ye are *dead*, and your life is *hid* with Christ in God', Col. 3:3.

But now is Christ risen from the dead, and, in Mark, a resurrection vision appears to the comfort of the once naked young man. And to others also, even to those, who, like Peter, weeping bitterly, can hardly forgive themselves, much less dare to hope for forgiveness from him whom they had denied and from whom they had fled in the hour of temptation.

'And very early in the morning the first day of the week'—
Mary Magdalene, Mary the mother of James, and Salome—
'came unto the sepulchre at the rising of the sun. And they
said among themselves, Who shall roll us away the stone from
the door of the sepulchre? And when they looked, they saw
that the stone was rolled away: for it was very great.'

'And entering into the sepulchre, they saw a young man
sitting on the right side, clothed in a long white garment; and
they were affrighted', Mk. 16:1-5.

Now this vision is peculiar to Mark: no one else records the
revelation. But what does it mean? Whatever it means, there
is no question but that the meaning is *unique to Mark*.

Observe the vision: 'a *young man*'. The Greek is *neaniskos*.
The last time this word occurred in Mark was hardly visionary:
it was wholly shameful. 'And there followed him a certain
young man', Mk. 14:51. This was that *neaniskos* who fled naked.

Observe that both young men—the naked defector and the
clothed visionary—I say, both young men are nameless, another
instance of the use of almost imperceptible inference in Mark.

But though both are nameless, one had no vision, the other
was the vision; one was of this world, the other was of the
world to come; one was this side of death, the other was the
other side of death. Of *Christ's* death.

The carnal *neaniskos* was running away from Christ's trial
and crucifixion, the visionary *neaniskos* was sitting at rest in
the place of Christ's resurrection: 'Sitting on the right side',
Mk. 16:5. So Christ 'sat on the right hand of God', Mk. 16:19.

The fleshly young man fled naked, but the spiritual young
man, having died with Christ, having been buried with him,
having risen in Christ's glory, sat at rest in accomplished
redemption: 'Clothed in a long white garment'.

The apostate young man in Mark 14:51 had the *sindōna*, or linen cloth, 'cast about'—Greek, *peribeblēmenos*, having cast about—his naked body: but there was nothing permanent about it, the garment was loose, it was an outward, transient show of a covering.

The young man in the vision, Mark 16:5, was also 'clothed' —*peribeblēmenon*, being cast about—but, in this case, clothed in the glory of Christ's resurrection from the dead.

The young man in the vision was clothed with 'a long white garment' which none shall take from him, nor can it ever be removed from about his body, being secured by the glory of Christ in the resurrection from the dead.

This resurrection vision was within the sepulchre 'hewn out of a rock'—Greek *petras*—and therefore hints at that spiritual house which, out of death, from the grave, in everlasting life, by the resurrection, Christ would build by the apostolic power so conspicuous in Peter: Greek, *Petros*.

Hence, 'With great power gave the apostles witness of the resurrection of the Lord Jesus', Acts 4:33, and the reason was, as the vision depicts, the apostles 'considered' the 'Apostle of our profession'.

And given such spiritual and inspired consideration of necessity the apostles pondered this same vision recorded in the gospel according to Mark, 'The beginning of the gospel of Jesus Christ, the Son of God', Mk. 1:1.

Notice that the visionary young man—at rest in Christ where he had once lain in death—appears as if risen from the dead. He sits at the right hand, the place of Christ's sheep. This is the choice, the elect place of the inheritance of the world to come. There the young man of vision rests in the light of the glory, beyond the reach of death, in the power of an endless life.

Neither had this young man of apostolic vision appeared of himself. He was no figure of those who thrust themselves by their own will into some so-called 'ministry' invented by carnal and worldly men.

This is a vision exclusive to the revelation of Jesus Christ, to one whom the Lord had chosen — 'He calleth unto him whom *he* would'; and, '*he* ordained twelve', Mk. 3:13,14.

The vision signifies—in that one young man—the vigour and continuance of the apostolic ministry which is called, ordained, and sent forth by the Son of God from the heavenly glory, in the anointing and power of the Holy Ghost below.

This is nothing, absolutely nothing, but nothing, to do with man. It is all to do with the Lord of glory.

Finally, observe the garment with which the young man in the vision was attired: 'Clothed in a long white garment.' In fact the word 'long' is mere interpolation: it does not exist in the Greek. It is an assumption on the part of the translators because of the nature of the garment.

Literally the Greek reads 'Clothed with a white robe'. But because a robe *is* a long garment, therefore the translators added the word 'long'. But why not translate the Greek with the single word 'robe', and let the garment speak for itself, as it did in the original tongue to contemporary Greek readers?

In fact the Greek word is *stolē*, robe. This is that resurrection garment, radiant with pure brightness, shining in the beauty of holiness, which clothed the young man in the vision.

This word, *stolē*, robe, is the noun form of a certain verb, *stellō*. *Stellō* is a complicated word having a broad range of meaning, of which we cannot now speak particularly.

However it is very necessary at present to notice that the verb, *stellō*, arises from precisely the same Greek root as the noun, *stolē*, robe. The *stolē* is that with which the young man was clothed in the vision.

Now, apart from drawing attention to the close and intimate connection between the two Greek words *stellō* and *stolē*, finally I bring to notice a certain preposition, meaning '*away from*'.

This preposition 'away from'—*apo* in the Greek—is often used in conjunction with Greek nouns or verbs, so as to form one new word of the two. The result is called a compound. Such compounds occur in the case of the verb *stellō*, and that of the noun *stolē*, translated 'garment' or 'robe'.

This results, respectively, in the compound words *apostellō* and *apostolē*. The latter, in English, is transliterated *Apostle*.

And Apostle, *per se*, is both the essence of Mark; the mystery in the tomb; and the continuity of the resurrection ministry. This apostolic ministry is what is preserved in glorious youthful vigour even to the end of the age.

Now this is the vision, just as it is the concept, of the gospel according to Mark.

PART TWO
THE STRUCTURE OF MARK

PART TWO
THE STRUCTURE OF MARK

T HE structure—or argument—which unfolds through the
sixteen chapters of this gospel is the means by which
Mark presents the *Concept* underlying the whole work.

Before so much as putting pen to paper the spirit of the writer
was filled with the glory of Christ viewed as the apostle of the
new testament.

By the Spirit of the Father, through the revelation of the
Holy Ghost, this glorious vision shone with heavenly radiance
within Mark's heart and mind. This *was* the concept.

But how was it to be conveyed? It was to be conveyed through
writing this gospel. From the beginning of the gospel.

Therefore, whilst broadly following the outline of the life of
Jesus, the entire composition of Mark's gospel has as its object
the conveying of its concept, not the conveying of the chronological history of the days of Jesus on earth.

59

Mark

The fabric of the material woven throughout the gospel according to Mark accords with this conceptional pattern, presenting its finished tapestry against the often hidden warp of the historical sequence of Jesus' pathway.

It cannot be overstressed that the matter — the text — is arranged to suit the vision, not the other way round. Hence, for example, Mark sublimely ignores Jesus' birth, childhood, and background, as if they did not exist. For his purpose—as with the record of Melchisedec—they did not. Then, here are warps which never surface in the finished pattern of Mark.

In this gospel the temptation *is* recorded, but nothing is said either of its form, or of its fasting. And yet things *are* said, which are to be found nowhere else.

To Mark, it is spiritually essential to the doctrine that John should appear to be put in prison before Jesus went forth to preach the gospel. Chronologically, however, this was not the case. Again, visits to Jerusalem are ignored—though many occurred—till that last and fatal going up to the city.

Parables, miracles, incidents, chronological sequence, all are rearranged to suit the doctrine, the concept. Here is no 'life of Jesus': here is the apostle of our profession.

The inclusion, exclusion, and arrangement of the events of Jesus' earthly life are ordered to reveal the *concept*.

What is not germane to this revelation is not in Mark. Only what is essential to it remains, and it remains not at all necessarily in historical sequence, but primarily in doctrinal consequence. On this basis the structure is developed, and to that structure or argument attention is now drawn.

I

The Coming of Christ and the Gospel
Chapters 1 to 4

i. Manifestation

M ARK opens with the unique statement 'The beginning
of the gospel of Jesus Christ, the Son of God', Mk. 1:1.
Mark records no genealogy, no beginning of days. We look in
vain for his birth; for Mary; for Joseph; for Jesus' infancy,
childhood, upbringing, or preparation. With an abruptness
that is unpreceded, he appears. He is made manifest.

Jesus Christ makes his appearance with the gospel, and he
makes his appearance as the Son. If so, the one enunciates the
covenant of which he is the apostle, and the other manifests
the advent of the mediator of the new testament.

There is no appeal to flesh and blood. No reference to the
most distinguished lineage and genealogy of all time. No appeal
to Israel; no appeal to the law; no appeal to Jerusalem. In a
word, no appeal.

His authority rests in the Sonship which he had with the
Father before the world was. His authority stands in his being
sent from God out of heaven, the mediator and apostle of
that covenant which eye had not seen, nor ear heard, neither
had it entered into the heart of man to conceive.

Nevertheless, of his coming, and of that covenant—or testament—all the prophets had borne witness.

Likewise the prophets had spoken of a messenger of God that should precede the coming of the Lord, to prepare his way. Here was the voice of one crying in the wilderness. But the context shows that this wilderness was much more than a geographical location. It indicates that all preceding and contemporary religion was in the sight of God as nothing save a barren, lifeless desert: a wilderness.

John did baptize in the wilderness, for there—spiritually—his voice must be heard, and there his message received.

His very clothing and meat declared the same, testifying of that solitary prophet sent of old, when the people aforetime had turned as one man from the living and true God. Yet—even then—God had reserved of the people a hidden remnant: seven thousand men who had not bowed the knee to Baal.

Just so there went out to John all the land of Judea, and they of Jerusalem, and were all baptized of him in the river of Jordan, confessing their sins. Among this mixed multitude, God's hidden remnant lay concealed.

To these John preached, saying, 'There cometh one mightier than I after me, the latchet of whose shoes I am not worthy to stoop down and unloose. I indeed have baptized you with water: but he shall baptize you with the Holy Ghost', Mk. 1:7,8.

At this point *for the first time* Mark introduces Jesus into the narrative: 'And it came to pass in those days, that Jesus came from Nazareth of Galilee, and was baptized of John in Jordan.' Straightway coming up out of the water, the mighty witness of God from heaven bore testimony to him.

Having, in a figure, passed beneath the floods of death at the hands of the law on behalf of a covenant people; having risen on their behalf; having secured their forgiveness and justification; having taken them in himself beyond the reach of the law, its curse, death, and the grave itself: What follows?

All heaven bursts open, and all deity conspires to declare the worth of God's beloved Son. At once appears the glory of the mediator, the apostle, and the sacrifice suited to the new testament, graphically depicted in the figure of the immersion of Jesus in the river of Jordan by John the Baptist.

Seeing that Christ did everything—in, of, and by himself—it is not *men* whom the Father addresses from heaven, nor is it *about* the Son that he speaks: it is *to* the Son that the Father's speech is addressed: '*Thou art* my beloved Son, in whom I am well pleased.'

With this declaration the Holy Ghost bore like witness, descending—in a figure—from heaven to abide upon the Son. This is Jesus Christ come in the flesh, whose way John had prepared, testifying, 'He shall baptize you with the Holy Ghost'.

Hence the sequence: first the sign of Jesus' submersion beneath the waters of death, borne down on behalf of transgressors by the condemnation of the law. Next his rising again. Then the opened heavens, signifying the anticipated ascension of the Son, having glorified the Father in his work on earth.

Immediately following the opening of the heavens, there appeared the descent of the Holy Ghost in a figure, witnessing that the ascended Son not only had brought in the new testament, but had received the promise of the Father for the entire covenant people of God, henceforth to baptize them by one Spirit into one body.

Finally, mark the witness of God to the Son, whose finished work had taken away the first to establish the second. The Father's voice from heaven testified to the perfected, the everlasting, the new testament, the covenant that stood—and would stand for eternity—between the Father and the Son.

All the Father's pleasure lay in his beloved Son, and every divine purpose and counsel was in and for the Son of his love. '*Thou art* my beloved Son, in whom I am well pleased.'

After so glorious a revelation as that of Jesus' baptism, it would be impossible for man to anticipate the next verse were it not *there*, plain for all to read: 'And immediately the Spirit driveth him into the wilderness', Mk. 1:12.

Immediately? After *that*? After the opening of the heavens; the descent of the Spirit; the Father's voice from the excellent glory, 'Thou art my beloved Son, in whom I am well pleased'?

Who could conceive the consequence directly following? The Spirit, just now descended in so signal a manner upon Jesus, in concert with the voice of the Father from the opened heavens testifying of everlasting love for the eternal Son, *immediately driveth him into the wilderness*?

The baptismal foreshadowing of Christ's death, resurrection, ascension, and glory, heralded with absolute confidence the redemption which he should accomplish when his ministry on earth closed *before that ministry had properly begun.*

The heavenly witness at Jesus' baptism *prejudged* the issue of what *now* lay before the Son in order that he should bring in the gospel.

There never was any question in the deity of the victory of the Son. Hence the baptismal testimony to that victory, not only before the battle was joined, but even prior to the adversaries being identified and described.

The coming triumphant ascendancy of the Son over all was in a manner already being celebrated in and by his baptism.

But any amount of witness from the certainty of the divine counsel could never in any way ameliorate or mitigate the suffering, humiliating pathway to be trodden by the feet of the Son, in order that his triumph should be established.

Hence, 'Immediately the Spirit driveth him into the wilderness.' That is, to set before him the Adversary and his powers, and to expose him to the formidable foes that stood between this threshold of his ministry, and his finally effecting the salvation of his people. *Thus* the battle should be joined.

As if to say, in facing the enemies at the place to which Jesus was driven, *This* is thy task. And by way of echo, to affirm to them by his being thrust by the Spirit to the seat of their presence and power, And *this* is your destruction.

Thus it was that in the frailty of his manhood the Son was driven immediately into the wilderness: 'Though he were a Son, yet learned he obedience by the things which he suffered', Heb. 5:8. For he was 'touched with the feeling of our infirmities', and 'in all points tempted like as we are, yet without sin', Heb. 4:15.

Nevertheless it was in this manhood that victory was to be won, and through such humanity that salvation was to be effected. Hence it came to pass after his baptism, *immediately* the Spirit driveth him into the wilderness.

Why? Because *there*, before his ministry commenced, he must first encounter the very foes he had come into the world, and into humanity, to conquer and defeat. To this end 'Immediately the Spirit driveth him into the wilderness', there to behold the enemies set in array to turn him from the enormity of his task.

He was to save his people from their sins; he was to take away their sin; he was to deliver them from wrath; he was to bring them beyond reach of both the law and its curse; and, moreover, he was to bring in an everlasting righteousness to be imputed freely to their account.

He was to redeem his people from this present evil world; he was to draw the sting of death; he was to overturn the victory of the grave; and he was to bring the chosen seed by way of resurrection from the dead to the inheritance of everlasting glory.

But none of these things could be done, whilst the vast and alien authorities that held man captive remained in power. Before anything else, *they* were the obstacle. There could be no new testament till every lawful question had been answered, all righteousness had been vindicated, and the entire demand of justice satisfied for time and eternity.

That granted, the enemies would have lost both power and authority, and their perpetual captives would have been released from bondage. It was the titanic struggle for such a victory that was in the minds of both Jesus and the adversaries, as, in the wilderness, for the first time, they met face to face.

The enormity of this task, I say, was set before the Son in the frailty of his human nature, alone with his foes in the wilderness. The lawful taking of their powers, the righteous destruction of each single enemy, was the paramount issue between Christ and his adversaries.

To break in pieces the gates of brass; to cut the bars of iron asunder; to loose the captives from the prison house; to deliver the prisoners from the old yoke of bondage: yes, but how should this lawfully be accomplished?

How, when such vast powers had reigned over mankind and the world, by the law of sin and death, unbroken since the Fall? How should these first be overcome and destroyed?

That was the question in the minds of the protagonists in the wilderness. For both knew that this enormous task must be fulfilled, *before* the Son of God could mediate and promulgate from the glory that new testament which he had come into the world to declare.

Such a new covenant must be founded upon eternal salvation vicariously effected, and unconditional justification freely given. Now, *that* is mediatorial and apostolic work, and to face the task Jesus was driven at the beginning into the wilderness.

There, alone, he was to measure the might of his adversaries; and there, alone, his adversaries were to measure the strength of the one who had come into the world to take away both their spoil and their place for ever.

It is a fact that to all intents and purposes many have dismissed the temptation in Mark as a kind of passing summary. Jesus' fasting is not mentioned; neither is the name 'Devil'—or, rightly, *Diabolos*—used.

There is not a word of Jesus' temptation concerning stones being turned into bread; nothing of his being shown all the kingdoms of the world in a moment of time; nor yet any mention of his being taken to the holy city, set on a pinnacle of the temple, and being urged to cast himself down.

Because all this detail belonging to Matthew and Luke adds up to a great deal more narrative than that found in Mark, generally little notice is taken of the latter account.

However this is to pass by a spiritual fountain of truth, simply because the well's mouth seems obscure. Indeed, few even *refer* to the temptation in Mark. Then who shall describe how *much* there is in Mark, narrated in so unique, striking, and suited a manner to the concept of this gospel?

Take the word 'driveth', where the Spirit 'driveth him into the wilderness'. It is not really 'driveth' at all. It is 'cast out'. The Greek is *ekballō*, a compound word formed by joining the preposition *ek*, 'out', 'out of', 'out from', together with the verb *ballō*, 'to throw or cast'.

It is from this Greek verb that we get the English 'ballistic'; as, for example, in 'ballistic' missile. Although Mark does not mention the name 'Devil'—*Diabolos*—the word *ekballō* does no more than substitute the preposition *ek* for *dia*, retaining the central verb *ballō*. A mysterious play on words for the perception of the spiritually-minded.

Next follows an extraordinary verse: 'And he was there in the wilderness forty days, tempted of Satan; and was with the wild beasts; and the angels ministered unto him', Mk. 1:13.

Cast out by the Spirit into the wilderness, in his spotless manhood he became exposed to the enemies for forty days. This is no question of fasting. Here it is a question of the exposure and trial of the moral worth of the one man—the second man, the last Adam—the man Christ Jesus, who could mediate, declare, and bring in the new testament.

Thus at the outset he was cast out alone in the worst of circumstances, in the face of the most terrible of enemies. Cast out, yes, but as if to challenge the foe, Do your worst.

By reiteration the verse emphasizes the environment: 'He was *there* in the wilderness forty days.'

Israel had wandered for forty years in the wilderness, a witness of their implacable unbelief. That wilderness, between Egypt and the promised land, signified the barren and dry waste of this present world, that is, as it pertained to the pilgrim and sojourner: 'I am a stranger with thee, and a sojourner, as all my fathers were', Ps. 39:12.

The wilderness therefore signified what the world had become to the tried people of God. The faithful among them looked for a world to come. They looked for another country, that is, an heavenly.

To such strangers, this world was alien, it gave them no nourishment, neither bread nor water. Life could not be sustained, unless nourishment came down from God out of heaven throughout the journey across this dry and barren waste to the promised land beyond Jordan.

Fallen Adam had been cast out of the fruitful garden, with his posterity banished in him, condemned to wander upon the earth which had been cursed for his sake. Shut out from the garden of God, nothing remained throughout the world but a lifeless wilderness even to the end of the age.

Moreover, in the nature of the Fall, this entire age of time—in which succeeding generations are born, live, and die—lay under the authority of *hostile* powers, the prince of which held mankind in captivity under sin and death.

It was into *this* environment, and before *those* powers, that the only man without sin since Adam fell was cast out by the Spirit to be tempted by the Adversary. He stood alone before the powers that had brought about the Fall and had reigned unchallenged over the world since the beginning of the age.

This was the wilderness in which Jesus was to be tempted of Satan.

In terms of *narrative*, only Mark uses the title *Satan*, and he uses it but once.

Both Matthew and Luke in their record of the temptation do use the name Satan, but in terms of quotation rather than their own narrative. Each uses the title once only, quoting the words of Jesus himself, 'Get thee hence, Satan', Mt. 4:10, and 'Get thee behind me, Satan', Lk. 4:8.

The narrative of Matthew refers to 'the devil'—more properly *Diabolos*—four times, and 'the tempter' once. Likewise Luke narrates the name *Diabolos*, but in this case five times. This is what the two evangelists themselves write, in the manner in which they record the incident.

Only when Matthew and Luke quote Jesus' own words do they use the name Satan, the sole name used, on the one occasion, in the narrative of Mark.

'The devil', *Diabolos*, is a Greek new testament term. Nothing like it exists in the old testament. It is not a proper name, but a descriptive title. It indicates a prosecutor or accuser at law, literally meaning 'One who throws or casts through', that is, casts accusations through a court of law to condemn the accused. This is the purpose of counsel for the prosecution.

Mark however uses the name Satan: 'And he was there in the wilderness forty days, tempted of Satan', Mk. 1:13. This title is rooted in the old testament. It is revealed first in the book of Job, and again particularly in the prophet Zechariah.

This is a title which refers back to the one who tempted Eve, caused the fall of Adam, and brought the whole world and all mankind under the rule of sin and death, cursed beneath the sentence of condemnation. It is in that sense the most ancient and revealing term or title.

This reign of sin and sentence of death remained unbroken until 'The beginning of the gospel of Jesus Christ, the Son of God', Mk. 1:1. Hence the unique and spotless Jesus, in the frailty of his manhood, was 'cast out' by the Spirit into the wilderness forty days, there to be tempted of Satan.

Now 'Satan' is a Hebrew word. It is not a proper name. It is a purely descriptive term. But it is used in Hebrew as the description of the arch-enemy. The word means Adversary. *The* Adversary.

In Mark nothing is recorded of the temptation itself: all that seems to be implied is confrontation. There is no word of 'The devil, taking him up into an high mountain, showed unto him all the kingdoms of the world in a moment of time', Lk. 4:5. Nothing about 'Then the devil taketh him up into the holy city, and setteth him on a pinnacle of the temple', Mt. 4:5.

None of this is in Mark. Not a word of the graphic and detailed scenes in Matthew and Luke. What is recorded in Mark is terse, spiritual, and allegorical. In place of the three temptations given at length in Matthew and Luke, Mark says simply 'And was with the wild beasts', Mk. 1:13.

Wild beasts? Where is the temptation in that? Few tell us. Does *anyone* tell us? Nevertheless Mark connects 'And he was there in the wilderness forty days, tempted of Satan' with 'And was with the wild beasts'.

If Mark does that, then there must be a spiritual significance in the connection, at least equal to 'The devil, taking him up into an high mountain, showed unto him all the kingdoms of the world in a moment of time', and 'The devil taketh him up into the holy city, and setteth him on a pinnacle of the temple'.

It is impossible that there could be *less* spiritual significance in the account of the temptation recorded in that gospel which soars to the heights of the concept of the divine and heavenly mediator and apostle of the everlasting covenant.

Then, in a context of Father, Son, and Holy Ghost; of the heavens being opened; of Jesus immediately being 'cast out' by the Spirit into the wilderness; of forty days of temptation by Satan; I say, of *that* and the wild beasts: Is it conceivable that the 'wild beasts', seen between Satan in one breath and angels in the next, should be intended to be other than spiritually interpreted?

71

How would mere animals add to the *temptation*? How could literal 'wild beasts' add to or subtract from the vast *spiritual conflict* upon which it is Mark's purpose to concentrate?

How could such things—following immediately after the mention of Satan—appear in Mark as *the equivalent* of the highly symbolic 'exceeding high mountain' revealing 'all the kingdoms of the world in a moment of time', and Jesus mystically being 'taken to Jerusalem' there to be 'set on a pinnacle of the temple'? Because the fact is, it *is* Mark's equivalent.

To take Mark literally, when 'all the kingdoms of the world in a moment of time', and elevation first to 'the holy city' then to 'a pinnacle of the temple', are clearly allegorical, is to ascribe a mysticism to Matthew and Luke denied to Mark.

This myopic literalization would force Mark into a comment —'with the wild beasts'—not only irrelevant in such a highly spiritual and momentous passage, but degrading: as if he inserted a phrase in such a weighty and divine context which would be nothing less than banal and little short of ridiculous.

'Wild beasts'? But then is it 'wild beasts'? In the original Greek it is not 'wild' beasts at all. That is what is so misleading to the spiritual.

Consider: In the context of the Fall; of the curse sounding throughout time upon the whole earth; of the unbroken reign of sin and death over all mankind; of the advent of the second man, the last Adam; of that unique manhood come forth to meet the Adversary, Satan, to overcome him *and his powers* on his own ground: What have wild beasts to do with it? Especially when *mistranslated*?

What? Are we supposed to take the mangled translation 'wild beasts' as if it were nothing other than literal? Satan is nowhere else connected with wild beasts. But elsewhere he is connected with *the* Beasts.

The Greek *thērion* occurs forty-six times in the new testament. The word means Beast. But the translators have failed to translate *thērion* consistently. Forty-two times faithfully they have given the correct rendering, Beast, or, in the plural, Beasts. This leaves four further references to *thērion*.

On one occasion, without the least authority, or the remotest textual reference, the translators render 'venemous beast' as the English equivalent of *thērion*, interposing the word 'venemous' at their fancy.

As to the three remaining occurrences of *thērion*, likewise the translators have intruded their own gloss into the English bible, adding to Beast the word 'wild' when no such adjective exists in the original.

Forty-six times the Greek *thērion* occurs in the new testament, and forty-six times the translation Beast should have enlightened the reader of the English bible as and when the word occurred.

In the case of Mark 1:13 to have added the word 'wild' when no equivalent appears in the Greek, commits a folly not only misleading in the extreme: it is downright mischievous.

The original is not 'tempted of Satan; and was with the *wild* beasts'. This deceptive *interpolation* inserted in Mark's text by the translators is nothing other than an attempt to 'rationalize' the spiritual by tampering with scripture.

Jesus was in fact 'tempted of Satan, and was with the beasts'. No 'wild' beasts about it. Also observe that there ought not to be a semicolon between the words 'Satan', and, 'was with the beasts'. It should be a comma. Why? Because there *is* a comma. And the reason for this is that the connection between the two is direct.

This connection—between Satan and the beasts—is not an isolated occurrence. It is to be found elsewhere.

Elsewhere we read of Satan and the beasts: the first beast; the second beast; those with the mark of the beast; the kings that reign one hour with the beast; the whore Babylon that sits upon the beast; the city Babylon that had the throne of the beast; and the false prophet of the beast.

Explicitly, these are the only references other than Mark 1:13 where Satan and the Beasts are connected. In Mark they are recognized and challenged. And in Revelation they are exposed and damned. And are these not the same? And is not this the like imagery? And to what can these refer other than to the same symbols of identical figures?

'And I stood upon the sand of the sea, and saw a beast rise up out of the sea, having seven heads and ten horns, and upon his horns ten crowns, and upon his heads the name of blasphemy.'

And what is the sea but the waters? And what are the waters but 'The waters which thou sawest, where the whore sitteth, are peoples, and multitudes, and nations, and tongues', Rev. 17:15.

And the beast rising out of these waters is that power, that world power, the power of the worldly state, and of world government, taking strength from the confluence of the waters which—mystically—gives rise to its formation. And what is this but 'All the kingdoms of the world in a moment of time'?

That is the first beast. But who gives him his existence, his power, and his time to reign? Who? 'The great dragon, that old serpent, called the Devil, and Satan.'

It is he—elsewhere called 'the god of this world'—who by his enticements, his deceptions, his delusions, exercises his power over all peoples in the Fall by means of the—symbolically described and allegorical—first beast.

But, Mk. 1:13, 'Beasts' is in the plural. There is another beast. 'And I beheld another beast coming up out of the earth; and he had two horns like a lamb, and he spake as a dragon.'

Two horns like a lamb? But Christ is the Lamb. Here is imitation. Spake like a dragon? The dragon is that old serpent, that is, Satan, who perverted the word and commandment of God whilst professing it, not to Adam, but to Eve. Here is subtlety.

This is the perversion of the truth. And who is the beast that comes out of the earth, earthy, working signs and wonders to deceive all nations concerning religion? This is nothing other than the power by which 'the devil taketh him up into the holy city, and setteth him on a pinnacle of the temple'.

By this power—under the figure of the second beast and false prophet—Satan rules by darkness and delusion over the whole religious world, and above all, over fallen Christendom. This is the power that reigns throughout the entire apostasy.

Now here is Satan with the beasts. And since both Matthew and Luke assure us that the temptation *was* in connection with the worldly state—all the kingdoms of the world in a moment of time—and this world's religion—Jerusalem below and an earthly temple—what is this other than the same thing as the mystical 'beasts' of Revelation?

And since it is certain that the book of Revelation uses the symbol of the beasts to signify the world state and earthly religion respectively, what shall we say of Mark, in a passage parallel with that of Matthew and Luke on the temptation?

What shall we say? That it is impossible that Mark would so much as *mention* mere animals in such a massively spiritual context. This in itself demonstrates that nothing else could be in mind with the expression 'Satan and the beasts' save the like spiritual reality figuratively conveyed.

Of course carnal translators—here less than honest—have slyly suggested mere animals by their impudent and unauthorized adding 'wild' to the scripture *thērion*, 'beast'. This deliberately leads the mind from the truth by inserting suggestive error. And it does so by tampering with holy writ.

These earthly-minded clergymen simply could not conceive of anything so spiritual—or allegorical—in Mark. But really it is no more allegorical or spiritual than the account of the temptation in Matthew and Luke.

Besides, we have shown how ignorantly—or rather, brutishly —Mark has been trampled upon by 'commentators' in the apostasy. Just as we have demonstrated that in reality the book is full of the most spiritual and almost imperceptible nuances, refined figures, and implied associations, the spiritual perception of which alone enables this gospel to be opened aright.

Another objection could be that *John* wrote Revelation, not *Mark*. Moreover, that there are no 'beasts' in the gospel according to John.

But this is easily answered: There is no *temptation* in the gospel according to John. Therefore of necessity Mark's 'Satan and the beasts' must draw from John's references in the book of Revelation, since his gospel has no parallel passage on the temptation, the Adversary, or his powers.

Tradition suggests that Mark wrote for Peter. I put no weight on tradition: scripture *itself* is complete. Nevertheless, if Mark *was* Peter's amanuensis, then Mark—through Peter—is necessarily connected with John. If so, Mark's reference to 'beasts' would find affinity with the same symbolism in John's Revelation.

Certainly Peter associates Mark with himself closely, I Pet. 5:13, and the intimate fellowship of Peter and John is clear throughout the gospels.

This is confirmed in Acts, where 'the boldness of Peter and John', Acts 4:13, standing as one for the gospel, hardly makes it difficult to believe that they should associate together in the symbol of beasts, even as they did in the reality of preaching the entire truth with one voice, Acts 3:1, 3:4, and 4:19.

What more fitting? If Mark be 'the beginning of the gospel of Jesus Christ', 'the Revelation of Jesus Christ' is certainly its conclusion.

If the only one able to challenge the unbroken reign of Satan and the beasts be 'cast out' in the weakness of his pure and perfect humanity that the enemies should thus be challenged to do their worst at the beginning, how fitting that these very enemies should be joined together under the same names and the like figures when they are to be destroyed by Christ in his glory at the end?

For it is certain, neither Satan, the first beast, nor the second beast, achieved anything in their temptation of the second man in the wilderness. Anything, that is, save the exposure of their own impotence and shameful malevolence manifest in its darkness by the radiance of the impeccable Overcomer.

Hence it is foretold at the last: 'And the beast was taken, and with him the false prophet that wrought miracles before him, with which he deceived them that had received the mark of the beast, and them that worshipped his image. These both were cast alive into a lake of fire burning with brimstone.'

'And the devil that deceived' the whole world 'was cast into the lake of fire and brimstone, where the beast and the false prophet are, and shall be tormented day and night for ever and ever.'

In the beginning of the gospel Mark taught that Jesus was cast out to be tried and tempted in the frailty of his divinely formed and unique humanity over the forty days, and, after those days, 'the angels ministered unto him'.

At the conclusion of the gospel in the book of Revelation John unfolds the way in which angels are central in ministering to Jesus Christ, fulfilling his commandment in the judgment and consummation of all things.

Again and again the seven angels usher in phase upon mounting phase, till, at the last, there appears the climax of the seven angels with the seven vials full of the wrath of God.

By these, Christ delivers and executes the everlasting sentence upon Satan and the beasts, consigning them to the vengeance of eternal fire, world without end. Amen.

The next two verses constitute the turning point in the early part of Mark's narrative: 'Now after that John was put in prison, Jesus came into Galilee, preaching the gospel of the kingdom of God, and saying, The time is fulfilled, and the kingdom of God is at hand: repent ye, and believe the gospel', Mk. 1:14,15.

This statement is like the two-leaved gates, up to which everything has led, and which now, opened, display the vista of the gospel stretched out before the reader, presently standing upon the threshold.

If anyone enquires, What caused these gates to open? I answer, the key words, 'Now after that John was put in prison'.

These words must be read spiritually. They cannot be read chronologically. They are out of chronology. Then they are to be interpreted spiritually. Something like an entire year is omitted between the last verse on the temptation, Mk. 1:13, and the following verse announcing John's imprisonment.

During this 'missing' year, historically it is a fact that Jesus and John ministered continually, though not in the same places. Jesus himself was found at Jerusalem, and in Galilee, preaching and teaching the gospel. John sustained his ministry the far side Jordan and thereabouts for at least twelve months. But all of this is ignored by Mark, as if it never happened.

By this the Holy Ghost signifies, that Christ and his gospel stand alone, not being revealed until the law and the prophets, Moses and Elijah, the old covenant and the earthly temple— having run their course — *have quite been shut out from view.* 'Now *after* that John was put in prison.'

In this context John is seen as the last of the old testament prophets, and the fading representative of that entire covenant.

Moses and Elias disappear from sight. No man is seen 'save Jesus only'. If so, the voice of the Son abides alone, even as he himself appears as the final speaker sent forth from God. Then of necessity we are to 'Hear *him*'.

But whilst the law is in view, whilst the old covenant is extant, whilst the killing commandment remains in force, *it is impossible to see Christ only and equally inconceivable to hear his gospel purely.* Hence first, in a figure, the entire legal system, the whole old covenant, must pass away. In a word, must be 'put in prison'.

Then, and not till then, the voice of the apostle of our profession will ring out singly and in a manner unique to the evangel, thence to echo in the heart of the hearers.

This is as true in experience today, as it was then. It is for this reason that Mark thus arranges the narrative by the Holy Ghost from heaven, in order to provide spiritual instruction for those with eyes to see and ears to hear.

Whence it follows that it is of the utmost importance to stress that *after* John was put into prison *then* 'Jesus came into Galilee, preaching the gospel of the kingdom of God'.

To imply that the 'Gospel of the kingdom of God' is another gospel than that preached after the ascension to every nation, as do the Dispensationalists—saying that the former was to the Jews only, and for Jesus' lifetime alone—is to fly in the teeth of scripture.

Mark had categorically assured us that he was writing 'the beginning of *the* gospel', Mk. 1:1. And if *the* gospel, then the definite article precludes the possibility of there being any other.

Besides, Jesus preached the gospel of the kingdom in *Galilee*—'Galilee of the *Gentiles*'—not in Judea or Jerusalem, the seat of the Jews. For God is not the God of the Jews only, but of the Gentiles also, Rom. 3:29,30.

Then what kind of perversion is this, and what is this *other*—Jewish—gospel, by which Dispensationalists cause Mark to contradict himself?

Have these people never heard Paul thunder, 'I marvel that ye are so soon removed from him that called you into the grace of Christ unto *another* gospel: which is *not another*; but there be some that trouble you, and would pervert *the* gospel of Christ. But though we, or an angel from heaven, preach *any* other gospel unto you than that which we have preached unto you, let him be accursed', Gal. 1:6-8?

It is perfectly true that Mark—to suit the concept—lays emphasis on *the* gospel as being that 'of the kingdom of God'. But this kind of distinction is no more—even less—than that used by Paul when he refers to 'the grace of Christ', and in the next breath calls the same thing 'the gospel'.

This mode of expression shows that in a given place the doctrine may require additional emphasis. This applies equally to the word 'gospel'. It may even go so far as to describe the gospel by different words altogether. There is no more to it than that: anything else is mere striving about words to no profit, II Tim. 2:14.

Just as the concept and context of Mark require the gospel to be qualified as that of 'the gospel of the kingdom of God', the like requirement compels Paul to say 'the gospel of Christ', Rom. 1:16; 'the gospel of God', Rom. 1:1; 'my gospel', Rom. 2:16; 'Christ's gospel', II Cor. 2:12; 'the glorious gospel of Christ', II Cor. 4:4; or 'the gospel of your salvation', Eph. 1:13.

The same principle applies to 'the gospel of peace', Eph. 6:15; 'the mystery of the gospel', Eph. 6:19; 'the faith of the gospel', Phil. 1:27; 'the word of the truth of the gospel', Col. 1:5; 'the hope of the gospel', Col. 1:23; 'the gospel of our Lord Jesus Christ', II Thess. 1:8; and 'the glorious gospel of the blessed God', I Tim. 1:11. Does this make fourteen gospels?

John, indeed, goes so far as to envisage an *angel* flying in the midst of *heaven*, 'having the everlasting gospel to preach unto them that dwell on the *earth*, and to every nation, and kindred, and tongue, and people', Rev. 14:6.

But, seeing that Paul affirms with all his strength that there is *one* gospel, and 'not another', John's vision is no more than an allegory consistent with the Revelation, just as 'the gospel of the kingdom of God' is a contextual description by Mark of the one, only, and singular gospel of Christ.

To say that Jesus preached 'the gospel of the kingdom' to the Jews, limiting that to the life of Jesus on earth, and teaching, as do the Dispensationalists, that *another* gospel was preached by the apostles after the ascension, is to make confusion worse confounded.

This is not only an heretical error which asserts *two* gospels—meanwhile cutting out vast parts of Matthew, Mark, Luke, and John from having any application to the *ecclesia*, or church—it is also a descent to the depths of blasphemy, by putting *another* gospel in the mouth of Jesus.

As if the gospel *itself* were not preached by Jesus, as Mark 1:1 assures us. Or as if the addition of the words 'kingdom of God' make it either less of a gospel, more of a gospel, or 'any other' gospel.

The gospel which was to be preached among all nations *after* Christ's ascension was one of 'repentance and remission of sins in his name', Lk. 24:47. This agrees perfectly with the words 'Repent ye, and believe *the* gospel', Mk. 1:15.

This is the *one* gospel, before described by Mark as 'the gospel of Jesus Christ, the Son of God', Mk. 1:1, and next as 'the gospel of the kingdom of God', Mk. 1:14. Immediately following this Jesus defines what he teaches as '*the* gospel' which they who heard were to repent and believe, Mk. 1:15.

As to Christ sending his apostles to preach *remission of sins* in his name following the ascension, What is this but the same gospel which he declared on earth, saying 'the Son of man hath power on earth to *forgive sins*', Mk. 2:10.

Such appalling error is incredible in men such as J.N. Darby and the Plymouth Brethren. I scorn to add the name of Schofield, who, with his second-hand plagiarism, feared not to add Dispensationalism to the words of this Book by incorporating his own writings, Rev. 22:18.

But even from the early days at Powerscourt the Brethren leaders together with other 'Evangelicals' were so taken up with fables about what they thought of as 'prophecy', that they quite lost sight of the integrity of 'the *beginning* of *the gospel*', inventing another gospel for the Jews only.

I say, Why should it seem a thing incredible with them that Jesus should preach his own gospel before he ascended? Why, especially considering that he preached it in the Spirit even before he became incarnate?

Otherwise, How was it that as a result of the preaching of the Son of God, thousands of years before his coming, Abraham was said to have been justified by faith, so that his faith was counted to him for righteousness, Rom. 4:1-5?

Seeing that faith comes by hearing, and hearing by the word of God, whose word was it that Abraham heard and believed, and who was the preacher of it, that the ancient patriarch should have been justified by faith two thousand years before the coming of Christ?

Indeed we are assured by him whose name is The Word of God, who was in the beginning, that 'the scripture, foreseeing that God would justify the heathen through faith, preached before *the gospel* unto Abraham', Gal. 3:8.

Likewise some one thousand years before Christ came, he preached in Spirit to David, who reported, 'The LORD said unto my Lord, Sit thou at my right hand', Ps. 110:1. Of this Peter assures us, saying that David spake before both of the resurrection and of the ascension of Christ, Acts 2:29-32.

And how could this be, had not Christ in Spirit preached forgiveness unto David, Rom. 4:6-8, and declared this to be the gospel of his salvation, by which he was justified by faith? And seeing that this was a thousand years before his coming, should Christ be expected to preach less, or preach another, than that gospel elsewhere described as *everlasting*? For if everlasting, then as immutable as it is singular.

From which truth confirmed in Abraham and David, it is evident that the entrance to the kingdom of God stands in the forgiveness of sins and free justification, by faith in the name of Christ, just as evangelical repentance is predicated to be the renunciation of all that prevents the embracing of the whole truth of the one gospel.

Now, the kingdom of God rests in righteousness, peace, and joy in the Holy Ghost. But if this be the case, then *the gospel* must be that by which the kingdom of God is entered, even as Jesus came preaching the gospel of the kingdom of God, and saying, The time is fulfilled, and the kingdom of God is at hand: repent ye, and believe *the* gospel.

Mark introduces Jesus into the narrative for the first time at his baptism, Mk. 1:9. But Jesus' first words—in Mark—are not recorded until Mk. 1:15: 'The time is fulfilled, and the kingdom of God is at hand: repent ye, and believe the gospel.'

As to the time being fulfilled, this refers to the day for which the antediluvian patriarchs waited; for which Abraham longed; and for which David — together with all the old testament saints—hoped. But, these all died in faith, not having received the promises, Heb. 11:13. At last, however, Mk. 1:9, the time was fulfilled.

With the coming of Christ came the preaching of the gospel, 'the revelation of the mystery, which was kept secret since the world began', Rom. 16:25. This was that which 'Eye hath not seen, nor ear heard, neither have entered into the heart of man', I Cor. 2:9.

In other ages this revelation was not made known unto the sons of men, Eph. 3:5, but now, saith Christ, 'The time is fulfilled'. With these words the gospel is introduced by the apostle of our profession.

Saith he, 'The time is fulfilled, and the kingdom of God is at hand: repent ye, and believe the gospel.' These are his first words as the apostle of the new testament.

However his first words are his present words, are his constant words, are his last words. The sum of his words is called, The gospel. This is what Jesus preached, Mk. 1:14, and about which he spoke, Mk. 1:15.

The gospel does not stand in signs, wonders, or miracles, although it was confirmed by them, both in Christ and in the apostles whom he sent.

The miraculous healings wrought by Jesus were the testimony of God that this was indeed the Christ, and that here was in truth the new testament. But neither Christ nor the new testament are to be confused with that miraculous testimony, as though they were the same thing.

The apostleship of Christ and the ministry of the new testament stand in nothing other than his preaching the gospel, first in its beginning in the days of his flesh, and finally in its fulness from the heights of his glory.

In the same way the reception of Christ and the new testament stand in repentance towards God and faith in the Lord Jesus Christ. Neither stands—or ever stood—in God's miraculous testimony to the coming, inauguration, or continuance of such blessedness.

The gospel of Christ, in which he declares the new testament, must never be confused with the wonders and miracles which confirm both speaker and speech. It is the gospel *itself* which saves.

Of the tens—perhaps hundreds—of thousands healed during the three years of Jesus' earthly ministry, How many *believed the gospel?* Of those made whole, Who did not later die and rot? Of those raised from the dead, Who was not buried again afterwards? How many were *saved* by the gospel unto *eternal* life beyond the grave, as opposed to the vast multitudes *healed* by his miracles in this present life *before* the tomb?

However many, it is a fact that from the total number who followed Jesus whilst he was alive on earth, all forsook him and fled at his being taken to be crucified.

Again, after his resurrection and ascension, certain gathered in the upper room. 'The number of names together were about an hundred and twenty', Acts 1:15. But these *had actually believed the gospel* not merely the *signs* of it. They had fastened on *the doctrine of Christ* not simply the miracles of Jesus.

Hence the apostle Paul says vehemently, 'I am not ashamed of *the gospel of Christ*: for it'—it; *it*; mark that: *it*—'is the power of God unto salvation to every one that believeth', Rom. 1:16.

This is the singular, the unique gospel, beginning with the testimony of John the Baptist, and concluding with Christ's return and its tremendous consequences. This is that *body of doctrine*, in its parts, and the sum of those parts, contained in the twenty-seven books of the new testament.

Miracles may have testified to Christ and his apostles, and the *ecclesia* under those apostles, but those miracles were in themselves nothing to do with believing the gospel. Indeed, they had fulfilled their function and ceased long before the close of the new testament scriptures. But the gospel itself—the only thing that saves—endures for ever. 'He that abideth in the doctrine of Christ, *he* hath both the Father and the Son', II John 9.

Hence the vast significance of Mark in presenting Jesus Christ the Son of God as the Apostle of the new testament. It is Jesus who first declared the gospel, making known the beginning of that doctrine of Christ without faith in which—'repent ye, and *believe* the gospel'—no one can be saved.

All the signs, wonders, and miracles recorded in the new testament point to this truth—this truth of the gospel—but not one, nor all, can either rival or supplant it, either in the beginning, the consequence, or the conclusion of the age: world without end. Amen.

Christ is the apostolic speaker; and his is the apostolic speech. The speaking is called, 'preaching the gospel'; and the speech, 'the gospel' itself.

The verb, *evanggelizō*, 'to preach the gospel', occurs in Matthew, Mark, and Luke. But the noun, *evanggelion*, '*the* gospel', belongs predominantly to Mark.

This is the apostles' doctrine. It is the doctrine of Christ. This is the new testament, and Christ is the apostle of it.

Evanggelion is not to *preach* the gospel: *that* would be the verb. But this is *the thing* itself: the *thing* preached: that is the noun. It is the doctrine of Christ in its sum, and in the parts comprising that sum.

Matthew used the noun four times. Mark doubles this, in half the space. Luke has no reference to the noun at all.

Others refer to preaching: that is everywhere. But—in the four gospels—when it comes to *what* is preached, the doctrine, the gospel itself, the weight and emphasis lies with that gospel whose very concept sets forth the Apostle of the new testament.

But then, given that concept, what else should one expect?

'Now as he walked by the sea of Galilee, he saw Simon and Andrew his brother casting a net into the sea: for they were fishers. And Jesus said unto them, Come ye after me, and I will make you to become fishers of men. And straightway they forsook their nets, and followed him', Mk. 1:16-18.

From this point onwards, the narrative quickens its pace. Jesus walks, first calling the brothers Simon and Andrew, and next the two sons of Zebedee.

Straightway the first brethren leave their nets, and the other brothers the mending of their nets. They follow Jesus immediately, departing on the one hand from their fishing, and on the other from their father in the ship with the hired servants.

The testimony of brethren not only stands in kinship: it is a witness also to sonship, and doubtless the concept of Mark's gospel is suggested by the Spirit through the incident of the calling of the brethren respectively. For it is evident that brotherhood and therefore sonship are of the essence in the new testament.

About a year prior to this calling of the brethren by the sea of Galilee, Andrew had heard Jesus, called his brother Simon, and had declared that they had found the Messias, which is, being interpreted, the Christ. In like manner this was almost certainly true of John, if not of his brother James.

There is no hint of this earlier encounter—perhaps twelve months before—in the gospel according to Mark. Given Mark's concept, the occasion of brethren, sons to the father, being called by Jesus—with its obvious spiritual suggestiveness and implication—takes precedence over mere historical data.

The allusions in this incident recording the calling of brethren, later to become the apostles of Christ in the new testament, provides a considerable range of allegorical teaching.

For example, there is the principle of separation. Not so much separation from evil, which demands repentance; or from unbelief, which faith requires: but separation from the ties of nature; the bonds of servitude; the yoke of the law;

and the futility of labour for life. These things may be hid from the carnal; but they are revealed to the spiritual.

'And they went into Capernaum: and straightway on the sabbath day he entered into the synagogue, and taught.'

The brethren whom he had called to follow him learned their ministry experimentally, observing Jesus as he walked; stood; and taught. They literally followed him as he declared the new testament in his own person.

The central feature of Jesus' apostleship was teaching, and is still teaching. As to that teaching, 'They were astonished at his doctrine: for he taught them as one that had authority, and not as the scribes', Mk. 1:22.

The scribes did teach, but they taught the dead letter of the law, 'understanding neither what they said, nor whereof they affirmed'.

They pointed to a sentence of death for a rule of life. They were blind to every ray of prophecy of a better testament to come, now embodied and sounding in their midst.

The scribes contradicted and confounded themselves, and, if so, where was *their* authority? They had no authority. Why not? Because their teaching was as void of understanding as it was empty of life.

Their ministry of the dead letter stood in the form of religion without the power. Their trust in dead works was full of presumption and self-righteousness.

Particularly, the scribes prided themselves in the service of their synagogue, above all on the sabbath day of rest.

But God had no rest in the scribes, their religion, their synagogue, or in their day. For death reigned over them, so that even the very demons slept undisturbed in the midst of their congregation.

But 'straightway on the sabbath day' Jesus 'entered into the synagogue.' The light of the glory attended his entrance, and the power of the gospel heralded his presence. This was the *new* testament.

This set forth the light against the darkness; it manifested the life against the deadness; it evinced the power against the form; and it contrasted the endless vigour in the new covenant over against the impotence of that which had waxed old and was ready to vanish away.

The entrance of Jesus into the synagogue, the power of the Spirit attending the apostle of the new testament, and the presence of God revealed in his Son, exposed that which had been undetected under the scribes' ministrations.

'And there was in their synagogue a man with an unclean spirit.' But what was a man with an unclean spirit doing in their synagogue? He was undetected. No one knew. Nothing existed in their dead and formal system to bring the man or the demon to light. But *now* everything came to light.

'Let us alone' cried out the demons, hitherto dormant whilst hearing the law in the synagogue every sabbath—all of which had never disturbed *them*—'What have we to do with thee, thou Jesus of Nazareth? art thou come to destroy us?'

Then spoke the deepest of them all: 'I know thee who thou art, the Holy One of God', Mk. 1:24.

The old covenant; the form of religion; the dead letter; divers ordinances and ceremonies; the keeping of sabbaths and days; the works of the law: all were impotent even so much as to detect the evil, let alone cast it out. In contrast, 'Jesus rebuked him, saying, Hold thy peace, and come out of him', Mk. 1:25.

'And when the unclean spirit had torn him, and cried with a loud voice, he came out of him. And they were all amazed, insomuch that they questioned among themselves, saying, What thing is this? what new doctrine is this?'

Why, this is the doctrine of Christ, the apostles' doctrine, the doctrine of the gospel, and it is the *power of God* unto salvation. Thus Jesus was made manifest, 'And immediately his fame spread abroad throughout all the region round about Galilee', Mk. 1:28.

'Forthwith, when they were come out of the synagogue, they entered into the house of Simon and Andrew, with James and John. But Simon's wife's mother lay sick of a fever.' Hearing of this, Jesus took her by the hand, and lifted her up. 'And immediately the fever left her, and she ministered unto them', Mk. 1:31.

'And at even, when the sun did set, they brought unto him all that were diseased, and them that were possessed with devils. And all the city was gathered together at the door', Mk. 1:32,33.

The whole of Capernaum, with its suburbs and environs, was crowded about the door of the house. For this same Jesus, the apostle of the new testament, had brought both house and kingdom of God nigh unto them. Indeed, he personified the house of God, so evidently did God dwell in him, and so signally did he testify of him.

The door of hope was opened in the person of the Son: he *was* the door, and by him, if any man entered in, he should be saved, and go in and out, and find pasture.

Of this the entire city was cognizant, amazed at the wondrous works of God as they thronged about the door. He himself was as it were a house of prayer for all peoples, and whatsoever they asked, he did it. And is not this the house of God? and is it not the gate of heaven?

As the setting sun gave way to nightfall, manifesting still that 'God was with him', Jesus 'healed many that were sick of divers diseases, and cast out many devils; and suffered not the devils to speak, because they knew him', Mk. 1:34.

Commanding the silence of demons, despising their testimony, at his rebuke they cowered and cringed in abject obedience, trembling before the manifestation of the power of God in the apostle of the new testament.

Now all these things which Mark recorded, from the time that Jesus went forth walking by the sea of Galilee until the gathering of the multitude about the door at nightfall, happened on one day. The sabbath day.

This was the day in which those in bondage under sin and death rested, hoping to please God by the works of the law. But Jesus wrought throughout that sabbath, till beyond sunset, and by this work he pleased the Father and brought the kingdom of God near to men: 'My Father worketh hitherto, and I work.'

Early in the morning, rising up a great while before day, Jesus went out, and departing into a solitary place, there prayed. This marks the apostle, and lies behind all apostolic ministry. And it does so continually: 'And Simon and they that were with him followed after him.'

I say, prayer distinguishes this ministry, so evident in the Son of God and his apostles. A life of prayer is equally apparent to this day in those ministers whom he ordains, who 'are with him' and 'follow after him', Mk. 1:36.

The brethren erred in seeking to constrain him, beseeching him to return to Capernaum for 'All seek for thee'. But he went forth into the next towns that he might preach in them also, 'For therefore came I forth'. And he preached in their synagogues throughout all Galilee, and cast out devils, Mk. 1:39.

And there came a leper to him, beseeching him, kneeling down to him, and saying unto him, If thou wilt, thou canst make me clean.

The leper was cut off from Israel; cast out of the temple of God; and condemned under the law. He was forbidden contact with the people of God. He had the plague. His clothes rent, his head bare, he was to cover his upper lip, condemned to wander, outcast and desolate, crying 'Unclean, unclean'.

Jesus, moved with compassion, put forth his hand, and touched him, saying, I will: be thou clean. As soon as Jesus had spoken, immediately the leprosy departed from him, and he was cleansed, Mk. 1:42.

Jesus required the judgment of the priest to be pronounced upon the cleansed leper, because the law was not yet fulfilled: 'Go, show thyself to the priest, and offer for thy cleansing those things which Moses commanded, for a testimony unto them', Mk. 1:44.

But why? Moses had not cleansed him; the law had not healed him. 'Those things which Moses commanded' would make him no more sound than the perfect wholeness which he had *already* received from Jesus.

A testimony to *them*? It may be so, but the overwhelmed man, transported with joy, filled with wonder, love, and praise, could not contain himself.

He knew by experience who had restored his health, he could speak of no one else, and of nothing else, he looked nowhere else, nor could he go beyond such perfection as he had seen in Jesus. And so it was that his testimony resounded throughout the countryside.

'He went out, and began to publish it much, and to blaze abroad the matter, insomuch that Jesus could no more openly enter into the city, but was without in desert places: and they came to him from every quarter', Mk. 1:45.

And what is this but that which was spoken of by the apostle Peter to Cornelius, saying, 'The word which God sent unto the children of Israel, preaching peace by Jesus Christ: (he is Lord of all).'

'That word, I say, ye know, which was published throughout all Judea, and began from Galilee, after the baptism which John preached; how God anointed Jesus of Nazareth with the Holy Ghost and with power: who went about doing good, and healing all that were oppressed of the devil; for God was with him.'

The close of the first chapter concludes the opening part of the narrative, having declared how Jesus was made manifest at the beginning.

Thus Mark opens the coming of Christ and the gospel. Jesus was manifested, yes, but no sooner manifested than opposed. The record of this mounting enmity occupies the next two chapters.

ii. Opposition

This section takes in the healing of the man sick of the palsy at the house in Capernaum; the calling of Levi and the feast at his house; the question of John and of the Pharisees concerning fasting; and the indignation of the Pharisees when they saw the disciples plucking corn on the sabbath day.

These incidents are followed by the healing of the man with the withered hand in the synagogue on the sabbath day; Jesus' withdrawal, and the gathering to him of multitudes from all countries.

Next appears Jesus' taking to a boat for the press of the throng round about him as he healed many; his prohibition of the unwanted testimony of unclean spirits; his going into a mountain to ordain the twelve, and their subsequent descent to enter into a house.

Thereupon Mark tells of Jesus finding no time to eat bread, and of his friends—or kinsmen—going out to lay hold on him, presuming him to be beside himself; also the accusation of the scribes from Jerusalem, and Jesus' exposure of their blasphemy.

Finally Mark records the coming of Jesus' mother and his brethren, calling him to come to them without, in response to which Jesus points to those who sat within, hearing his word. These did the will of God, and these he refers to as his brother, his sister, and his mother.

This summarizes the entire passage on opposition, ending at the close of chapter three. Now consider that opposition.

Beginning at Mark 2:1, Jesus entered into Capernaum, there to be found in the house of the brethren—a reference unique to Mark, and an allusion too significant to ignore. This was noised abroad. Straightway many were gathered together, so that there was no room to receive them, no, not so much as about the door: and he preached the word unto them.

And four came, bearing a litter on which lay one sick of the palsy, but they could not come near to him for the press of the crowd at the door. However, finding the throng less dense elsewhere, they ascended to the roof, which they broke up, and, having done so, let down the bed on which the sick of the palsy lay. This was seen by all in the house.

When Jesus saw the faith of the four, he said to the sick of the palsy, Son, thy sins be forgiven thee. It is this overwhelming kindness that brings out the beginning of the opposition in Mark. 'But'—notice the But—'there were certain of the scribes sitting there.'

These seated scribes were out of the blessing, and, if so, they were under the curse, for it is written, Blessed is the man that walketh not in the counsel of the ungodly, nor standeth in the way of sinners, nor sitteth in the seat of the scornful. In this place those scribes sat, adopting the posture of the scorner, and finding fault with the words which Jesus spoke.

The scribes assumed a place of lofty detachment, from which they might look down censoriously, in order to judge both the word and power of Christ's gospel. This is called 'reasoning in their hearts', Mk. 2:6.

Mark does not say, Reasoning in their minds. Their reasoning was not in their minds; it lay at the root of their enmity, the heart. But 'immediately when Jesus perceived in his spirit that they so reasoned within themselves, he said unto them, Why reason ye these things in your hearts?', Mk. 2:8.

They had heard—even seen—the testimony of God to Christ and his gospel, the unprecedented signs and miracles which he had wrought, the wonders done not to just a few, but to vast multitudes. What was there to reason about? Nothing. It was all abundantly clear: more than clear.

But filled with envy and malice in their hearts they sought out how to condemn Jesus. But they would in no circumstances admit their inward enmity, much less seek that their hearts should be healed. So they judged him: 'Why doth this man thus speak blasphemies? who can forgive sins but God only?'

Jesus posed a question. They should choose between two statements. Whether is it easier to say to the sick of the palsy,

Thy sins be forgiven thee; or to say, Arise, and take up thy bed, and walk?

Now, of these statements, Jesus had already uttered the first. It was that utterance —'Thy sins be forgiven thee'— which caused the scribes to reason in their hearts. However, anyone in the crowded room could have *said* that, simply because *no effect followed visibly.* It was easy to say.

But that was not so with the second statement—'Arise, and take up thy bed, and walk'—the immediate consequences of which would be apparent to all. That was not easy to say.

Who could—who dare—say such a thing before the multitude? Since nothing would happen, no one would put himself in the place of being ridiculed for so outrageous a folly.

But, if the sick of the palsy *should* rise up when Jesus spoke these words, what other testimony could they require? This *must* be the Christ, the apostle of the new covenant, with power on earth to forgive sins.

Then said Jesus, 'That ye may know that the Son of man hath power on earth to forgive sins, (he saith to the sick of the palsy,) I say unto thee, Arise, and take up thy bed, and go thy way into thine house. And immediately he arose, took up the bed, and went forth before them all', Mk. 2:9-12. Now where was their reasoning? As to the multitude, 'They were all amazed, and glorified God, saying, We never saw it on this fashion.'

And Jesus went forth again by the seaside, teaching the multitude which resorted to him. Passing by he saw Levi, and, apparently without stopping, said, 'Follow me'. Just that: but it was the inward mighty power of the apostle of the new testament that wrought with these two words, and, without hesitation, Levi arose, left all, and followed him.

And it came to pass that as Jesus sat at meat in his house, many publicans and sinners sat also together with Jesus and his disciples, for there were many, and they followed him.

Now appears the second incident of opposition, in which the Pharisees joined the scribes, criticizing Jesus behind his back to the disciples. This was because Jesus and his disciples ate and drank with publicans and sinners. However it was not to join them, but to save them, Mk. 2:17.

On the other hand the disciples of John the Baptist and of the Pharisees—who used to fast—came face to face with Jesus, not to judge Jesus' disciples for eating and drinking indiscriminately, but for eating and drinking at all: 'Why do the disciples of John and of the Pharisees fast, but thy disciples fast not?', Mk. 2:18.

Why did Jesus' disciples fast not? Because the bridegroom was with them.

And, seeing that the bridegroom had come at last—of whom Moses and all the prophets testified—it followed that the winter was past, the rain was over and gone; the flowers appeared on the earth; the time of the singing of birds had come.

The voice of the turtle was heard in the land; the fig tree had put forth her green figs, and the vines with the tender grapes gave a good smell.

For the time was fulfilled. This was the time of joy and gladness and not a time of mourning and fasting. The heavens rejoiced, and earth rang again with joy. The kingdom of God had come, God had borne witness, and Jesus Christ had been manifested. And shall these people *fast*?

The next occasion of opposition discovers the Pharisees finding fault with the disciples to Jesus himself. Not long previously they had criticized Jesus behind his back to his disciples, and now they criticize those disciples behind their backs to Jesus. 'Behold, why do they on the sabbath day that which is not lawful?', Mk. 2:24.

The disciples plucked corn to eat on the sabbath day. Fault was found not with the hungry disciples for plucking corn as such, but that they did this on the sabbath day.

So that first they are wrong for not fasting, and now they are wrong for eating. What would satisfy these critics? Some strange dichotomy in which the disciples starved to death from fasting whilst at the same time they perished from gluttony? Only provided, of course, that they avoided dying on the sabbath.

'And Jesus entered again into the synagogue; and there was a man there which had a withered hand. And they watched him, whether he would heal him on the sabbath day; that they might accuse him', Mk. 3:1,2. Observe that Mark's comment explains their motive: 'that they might accuse him.'

They sat there: they watched him. They waited to see if the miraculous power of God should break forth from heaven upon earth at his sole word, for they knew of him what was so conspicuous by its absence from themselves: that he would pity the afflicted.

And if it was so; if God should work so astoundingly; then, it being the sabbath, they would blame Jesus for working. But it would be *God* who was working. If not, How could it be done?

'And when he had looked round about on them with anger, being grieved for the hardness of their hearts, he saith unto the man, Stretch forth thine hand. And he stretched it out: and his hand was restored whole as the other. And the Pharisees went forth, and straightway took counsel with the Herodians against him, how they might destroy him', Mk. 3:5,6.

Mark

This is the fifth occasion of opposition in as many incidents recorded by Mark. What started by silent reasoning in the heart, spread to backbiting to his disciples, increased to complaints against his disciples to Jesus twice running, reached its culmination in watching to accuse him, and, finally, plotting his murder.

To this end — conspiring to murder Jesus — the Pharisees consulted with those whom they despised: the Herodians.

The Herodians had access to and influence with the secular powers and state authorities, who were well able to find cause to put him to death officially. This was reason enough for the Pharisees to drop their fastidious scruples and join cause with those whom they despised, and with whom they would otherwise have had no dealings.

'But Jesus withdrew himself with his disciples to the sea: and a great multitude from Galilee followed him, and from Judea, and from Jerusalem, and from Idumea, and from beyond Jordan; and they about Tyre and Sidon, a great multitude, when they had heard what great things he did, came unto him', Mk. 3:7,8.

So that despite the opposition and the current plotting for his death, the increase of God so much the more abounded.

So great was the throng pressing upon Jesus on the sea-shore that 'he spake to his disciples, that a small ship should wait on him', the multitude leaving him no space to stand on the shore because of their pressure to reach him.

'For he had healed many; insomuch that they pressed upon him for to touch him, as many as had plagues.'

'And unclean spirits, when they saw him, fell down before him, and cried, saying, Thou art the Son of God. And he

100

straitly charged them that they should not make him known', Mk. 3:11,12. He would have none of their recognition, nor would he brook testimony from such a quarter.

'And he goeth up into a mountain, and calleth unto him whom he would: and they came unto him. And he ordained twelve, that they should be with him, and that he might send them forth to preach, and to have power to heal sicknesses, and to cast out devils', Mk. 3:13-15.

This is the beginning of the apostolic ministry ordained by the apostle of the new testament.

From that commencement—though without the distinctions peculiar to the twelve—and upon precisely the same principles, to this day Christ from the heavenly glory continues to exercise his sole prerogative in sending his ministers.

This appears, for example, in First Timothy. Note also that such an apostolic gospel leads to and results in 'the house', cf. Mk. 3:19 and I Tim. 3:15. Likewise read the book 'First Timothy'.

'And the multitude cometh together again' — about the house—'so that they could not so much as eat bread', Mk. 3:20. 'And when his friends heard of it, they went out to lay hold on him: for they said, He is beside himself.'

Now here is obstruction; and it is the first sign of it from Jesus' 'friends' or 'kinsmen'.

But a man's foes *shall* be those of his own household, and it is inevitable that, in the midst of one's family, opposition shall rise up sooner or later.

He is mad—beside himself—said his kinsmen, who would lay hands upon him, no doubt to restrain him in the madhouse.

But it is they that are mad. But what can be expected of fleshly relations? These cannot be brethren, for they are not born of the Spirit, but, being fleshly, they are born of the flesh.

The biblical scholars, scribes in the dead letter, come down from Jerusalem, to inform his friends, kinsmen, and all others of what they affirm to be the source of Jesus' madness.

'He hath Beelzebub, and by the prince of the devils casteth he out devils.' It is evident, they must somehow account for the wonderful works wrought by him, and, therefore, they ascribe what he did to the prince of the demons, as if by them he did miracles and cast out devils.

Here is the sixth occasion of opposition, and in essence the worst. This was the verdict passed upon Christ and the gospel from the holy city, the chief priests, the rulers, elders and scribes: It was all of the devil: Satan was the source.

But if Satan casts out Satan, it is all one as if a man should cut off his own arms and legs: and what man is so stupid as that?

Besides, would he who had deceived the whole world, and brought down all humanity, harm himself in a way that no sane—or even insane—man would do?

What kingdom at peace with itself would deliberately foment civil war, to rend itself in pieces, when all had been calm? Or what members of a household, once tranquil, would turn and attack one another without reason? what would be left of the household? No more would Satan turn and rend his house, or divide his own kingdom.

It was not Satan, but the Holy Ghost through whom Jesus had wrought. Then, by ascribing the power and work of the Spirit to Satan, they blasphemed the Holy Ghost. This has no forgiveness, either in this life, or in that to come. Such accusers are in danger of eternal damnation.

'Because they said, He hath an unclean spirit', Mk. 3:30. But he had the Holy Spirit.

However, Jesus' mother and brethren, taking fearful notice of so solemn a sentence from the holy city, indited by the highest religious authorities, duly delivered by the scribes—the biblical scholars—from Jerusalem, hope to reason with Jesus. Hence, in awe of religion lawfully established, they send for him to come to them.

'There came then'—note that, 'then': that is, when *they* said, 'He hath an unclean spirit', Mk. 3:30—'There came *then* his brethren and his mother, and, standing without, sent unto him, calling him', Mk. 3:31.

But what were they doing *without?* that is, *outside?* Being without, they heard the blasphemous mischief of evil speakers, which, had they been within, would never have come to their ears.

Standing without? There is no blessing in that. Blessed is the man who standeth not in the way of sinners. For the blessing does not rest upon those standing without, but upon those sitting within. These heard his word, which hearing is called, Doing the will of God. But standing without was not doing the will of God.

Standing without 'Calling him'? What, calling him from preaching the word within? And who were *they* to call *him?* Moreover, to call him from the work God sent him into the world to fulfil?

By so doing they would hinder the work of God on the basis of fleshly relationships, and all because they feared the scribes and the system which sent them.

Because the fear of man was the cause for which his mother and brethren stood without, calling him.

This is the seventh, and last, occasion of opposition, encompassing the entire range to which he was exposed, perfectly opening the manner in which he was hindered.

'And the multitude sat about him, and they said unto him, Behold, thy mother and thy brethren without seek for thee', Mk. 3:32.

'And he answered them, saying, Who is my mother, or my brethren? And he looked round about on them which sat about him, and said, Behold my mother and my brethren! For whosoever shall do the will of God, the same is my brother, and my sister, and mother', Mk. 3:33-35.

This concludes the chapter, besides the passage expounding the nature of the opposition to Christ and the gospel. Given the living, vital and real presence of the apostle of the new testament, one of two things must follow.

Either one hears his voice, and, sitting at rest in the house, receives his doctrine, in which case there is joy and gladness, and he is embraced.

Or one hears the voice of his enemies, and, standing beyond earshot outside the house, contends with his doctrine, in which case there is confusion and darkness, and, sooner or later—if remaining unjudged—opposition and hatred.

iii. Revelation

Chapter four concludes the passage on The Coming of Christ and the Gospel. This closing section is a prophetic revelation of immense range and penetration. It views the apostolic ministry of Christ from the time at which he was speaking, soaring over and above the age, not concluding until the last day at the end of the world.

This is revelation: the parables themselves are a revelation. But revelation must attend the parables. Hence Jesus admonishes 'He that hath ears to hear, let him hear'. Teaching is being revealed which must be drawn deeper than the natural faculties in order to grasp the spiritual meaning. In and of itself this requires a work of personal and inward revelation.

Such revelation must attend the parables if they are to be effectual. There is a within and a without in this matter: 'When he was alone, they that were about him with the twelve asked of him the parable', Mk. 4:10. Then he revealed it to them inwardly.

But as to those who were outside, 'Without a parable spake he not unto them', Mk. 4:34. The parables were a revelation in and of themselves: those outside recognized that. But beyond that recognition there was nothing personal, experimental, or inward.

However, sharing that recognition, but transcending it, everything *was* personal, experimental, and inward to his own, separated to him within. 'When they were alone, he expounded all things to his disciples', Mk. 4:34.

Simply grasping that the parables were themselves a revelation did not of itself disclose the hidden mystery which lay beyond their wording. This deeper revelation lay in God's prerogative, and stood in his own election. 'Unto *you* it is *given* to know the *mystery* of the kingdom of God: but unto them that are without, all these things are done in parables', Mk. 4:11.

Of this those that were without could not complain: Jesus received them, he taught them, he declared the outward revelation of the parables to them, and they heard them.

Of what then could they complain? They had received everything that their heart desired.

But for all that, 'Unto them that are without, all these things are done in parables: that seeing they may see, and not perceive; and hearing they may hear, and not understand; lest at any time they should be converted, and their sins should be for-given them', Mk. 4:11,12.

These were the multitude, the greater number of hearers that attended Jesus. But despite this attention, they neither saw, nor heard, nor were converted, nor were their sins forgiven them.

These sought after the flesh, and by the flesh they owned the exterior revelation which they had heard.

Nevertheless — apart from these — God was calling out a people after the Spirit, and by the Spirit that outward revela-tion was secretly and inwardly revealed to the hidden and interior man of the heart.

These chosen disciples, eschewing their own sight, hearing, knowledge and ability, were drawn to Jesus when he was alone. They came about him with the twelve, within, and, because the voice of the Son of God had penetrated their inward spirit, they both perceived and understood, they were converted and their sins were forgiven them.

And this they had by the revelation of Jesus Christ the Son of God, from his Father in heaven, so as inwardly to hear his spiritual voice, receiving his apostolic ministry by the power of the Holy Ghost.

Although the parables are called teaching—'he began again to teach', v. 1; 'he taught them many things by parables', v. 2— nevertheless this does not refer to the substance or body of his doctrine—which is called the word, or the seed—but to his manner of delivering it.

That is, the parables teach the *way* in which Jesus delivers or sows the word, or seed.

Although at this juncture only three parables are recorded in Mark—as opposed to seven in Matthew—yet these three are enough to convey the most graphic and comprehensive revelation of the course of the apostolic testimony throughout the age.

The parables do not speak only of Jesus' teaching to those people at that time. It is perfectly clear that by using the *circumstances* of his then current activity, the prophetic revelation soars above the contemporary period and scene to speak of things to come which hold good throughout the age.

The parables—together with relevant exposition and admonition—take up the first thirty-four verses of Mark chapter 4.

In these verses there are twenty-three references to the apostolic ministry of Christ, describing his teaching in seven different forms. There are fourteen references to hearing, all alluding to the hearing of faith. The law and its works are conspicuous by their absence. The fourteen references to hearing take four grammatical forms.

By far and away the most prominent, detailed and expanded parable is that of the Sower. Not counting the first two verses—the setting for the whole—the Sower takes up eighteen verses.

Out of a total of twenty-three references to Jesus' teaching in the parables, thirteen of these appear in the parable of the Sower. This figure does not include the first two verses.

Of the full number of fourteen references to hearing, nine occur in the parable of the Sower. The significance attached to this parable is therefore made abundantly clear.

107

The twenty-three references to the apostolic ministry of Christ in the thirty-four verses encompassing the parables fall into seven categories.

There are two references to Jesus' teaching; one to his doctrine; seven times the term parable occurs; and once the narrative speaks of his expounding. Jesus speaks twice of the kingdom of God; once of the mystery of the kingdom of God; and nine times he refers to the word.

The spiritual and interior response to any and all of these is hearing, to which there are fourteen references in all, presented in four different grammatical forms.

Once hearken occurs; once hearing; twice heard; and ten times the word hear appears.

There are no references at all to works or doing. These belong to the old covenant. All the working and doing in the new covenant is of God, not man.

The setting of the parables must be viewed as figurative. Although Jesus *did* sow the seed at that time among the Jews, nevertheless, the seed proper is that of the whole gospel, and not just its beginning.

Hence it is after his death, resurrection, and ascension, with the consequences of justification, sanctification and redemption, that the fulness of such a seed must appear. Then, it is sown from glory, it is given in the power of the Holy Ghost, and it follows the reception of Christ into heaven.

This is fact. Whatever objection anyone may feel about allegorizing the setting, it can never alter the fact that what Jesus was doing *then* in part, was what he would do in fulness from the ascension.

This is seen in the last chapter of Mark. It is why unbelievers would obliterate the last twelve verses of Mark. But since the parables teach the *way* in which Christ ministers the gospel from the glory, and the consequences of that ministry throughout time, the spiritual reader would *expect* both a recorded ascension in Mark 16 and an allegorical setting in Mark 4.

Consider. Jesus is not on the land. Literally he is not standing upon earth. It is the multitude that is standing upon earth. 'He entered into a ship, and sat in the sea'—though literally buoyed up above it—'and the whole multitude was by the sea on the land.'

Here is a figure of the Lord having departed from the earth. The whole multitude was on earth, but he was not. In a figure he was separated from all mankind, and, one could say, by the waters of death: he was on one side, and they were on the other.

Christ may thus be seen as risen, ascended, and seated over all. Because it is actually *true* that from this position the real sowing of the full gospel began. That is what is being depicted.

To be a suitable figure of what follows, this *must* be depicted. His position at *that* time set forth—in the only way possible— the Lord ascended into his glory: 'Sit thou on my right hand'. Thence he should commence the heavenly sowing.

As to mankind, the people are portrayed as standing—a posture of waiting—to show forth the consequences—one way or the other—of the heavenly Sower broadcasting the seed to fall from above upon the earth.

At the time of the parables, it was 'touch me not: for I am not yet ascended'. But, once ascended, the sowing became heavenly, divine, and mysterious, accompanying the labourers whom he sends. It is not his audible voice to natural ears, or his physical presence to carnal sight: it is his speaking by the Spirit to the hidden man of the heart.

Wherefore it is the vision of faith to see him who is invisible. This is the apostolic and heavenly ministry of the Son of God from the glory. Thus his position then, in that contemporary setting, presented a figure of the coming reality.

The three parables in Mark view the entire epoch from different aspects. The greatest emphasis is laid upon the parable of the Sower, which is the only case where, alone with his disciples, Mark gives Jesus' own explanation of what he had taught.

The second parable, that of the Seed, is unique to Mark. The last is that of the Grain of mustard seed. There is a natural and proper sequence to the three.

The key to the interpretation of these parables is discovered by determining how each is related to time itself. The parables view time from three different aspects.

The figure depicted in the parable of the Sower is to be seen as recurring throughout the age. There was not one sowing once. The sowing is to be repeated generation by generation. So that many such sowings occur again and again throughout the passage of time.

The contrary is the case with the second parable. Here it appears as if the whole of time were contracted between one sowing and one harvest. The entire age is shrunk to but the seasons of a single crop. The parable is as a glass which reflects the entire epoch from the advent to the coming again of Christ, when time shall be no more.

Such a vision embraces no more than one sowing at the beginning, one period of growth, and one harvest at the end of the world. One sowing: one harvest.

The parable of the Grain of mustard seed is to be considered in terms of the development of history. From the day in which

Christ began his apostolic ministry, unfolding through the phases of this era, comprehending the astounding changes wrought throughout time, the passage of history ushers in the final scene that remains at the end of days.

But to return to the parable of the Sower. The Sower is Christ himself. 'See that ye refuse not him that speaketh *from heaven*' resounds across the firmament to echo again and again upon earth to the end of the age, as the apostolic and heavenly Sower successively broadcasts the seed to each generation.

This is no single period, or any one generation: it is *now*. '*To day* if ye will hear his voice, harden not your hearts.' It is his present work, and, all may be assured, he is doing that work to this moment.

However, though sown on the wayside, shallow, thorny, and good ground, the seed survived and flourished in but one instance. Consider the threefold loss of the seed, as opposed to the single gain: What caused the difference in the issue?

Not the Sower who sowed the seed: he broadcast equally, whether the ground were wayside, shallow, thorny, or good. Not the seed which he sowed: that seed was precisely the same no matter where it fell.

Then what caused the difference in the issue? The difference lay in the state of the ground *before* the sowing. If so, everything depended on preparatory work.

Where this was good—*prior* to the falling of the seed from the hand of the Sower—the thirtyfold, sixty, or hundredfold yield from such ground was already assured.

Where the wayside was impenetrable, the stony ground shallow, or the thorny ground uncleared, the disastrous result was inevitable from the beginning. Rather, from *before* the beginning.

111

All this depicts the necessity of a prior work of God—a 'law work' as the old divines put it—without which there could be no fruit: only barrenness and death.

Regarding the next and perhaps most visionary parable—unique to the gospel according to Mark—that of the Seed, but one sowing occurs throughout the whole of time.

At the beginning it appears that a man had cast seed in the ground at the season of sowing. As the age unfolds, it is as if he should sleep, rising night and day, and the seed should spring and grow up, he knoweth not how.

For the earth bringeth forth of herself; first the blade, then the ear, and then the full corn in the ear. This takes time, it follows the seasons, and it is inevitable.

But when the fruit is brought forth, immediately he putteth in the sickle, because the harvest is come. The harvest is the end of the world.

Here, the whole age is but the season between sowing and reaping. Moreover, in this parable, all the seed—and hence the ground—is good, bearing fruit accordingly.

It is the Lord's harvest, just as *he* purposed it in his mind before the beginning. All is from a divine view, bringing out the single harvest of the resurrection of the just.

This harvest constitutes all that the apostle of the new testament ever sowed in God's prepared good ground, as if it were all sown at once. Thus at last the harvest shows the entire fruit of his labours.

Here are no tares: that is another view, not in Mark. Here is no separation of good from bad; that belongs to Matthew. The lost seed in the threefold worthless ground is not considered.

Here is the absolute success of the apostle of our profession from the first day till the last. Out of all time, at the end of time, the harvest constitutes all that he intended, just as he had intended it, and wholly for himself. 'Christ the firstfruits; afterward they that are Christ's at his coming.'

Finally there is the parable of the Grain of mustard seed. This also commences with the sowing of the seed. But, like the husbandmen in Israel of old, here is the history of what religious men, professing Christians, the systems of Christendom, progressively effect by taking over the things of God.

With the passage of time there is a complete change of character from the original, ultimately forming a gross aberration, swarming with foreign elements. This bears no resemblance to what had been intended at first.

How did this happen? Because of a total lack of husbandry. Nature had been allowed to run riot by the indolence of the husbandmen. And so it has come to pass.

It should be observed that the apostolic ministry of Christ from the glory, even to the end of the age, emphasizes one activity and one only: that of teaching. The seed is *the word*.

There is no suggestion of the continuation of those inaugural miracles that accompanied the ushering in of the new testament, just as they did that of the old. The *twenty-three* references to Jesus' teaching show that the *gospel of Christ* is the power of God unto salvation, just as it is *the truth* that sanctifies: 'Thy *word* is truth.'

If there *were* any question of an age-long application in the parables to signs and wonders, by interpretation it would lie in the signal and wondrous way in which the seed sprang up with such astonishing speed in the case of the shallow-ground hearers.

But that wonder lay in the eye of the beholder, and, to the instruction of all, it did not—for it could not—last the season.

The vital lesson of the parables is that the whole of salvation stands in sowing and growing, and, at that, in good ground alone. This is no opinion. It is the overwhelming testimony of the apostle of our profession.

In the same way, what appears in those in whom the seed is sown is hearing. This is repeated fourteen times over, and nothing else is looked for whatsoever. It is this that bears the fruit, in and of itself.

'Received ye the Spirit by the works of the law, or by the hearing of faith?', Gal. 3:2. 'Faith cometh by hearing, and hearing by the word of God', Rom. 10:17.

Miracles, signs, wonders, astounding second experiences, supernatural gifts; none of these is mentioned. He that hath ears to hear, let him hear. It is *hearing*, the hearing of faith, for which the apostle of the new testament looks, and which he finds in the good ground, throughout the entire age.

There is no place for works of any kind, and neither has the law or a past covenant any place in this matter. Here are *facts*, not prejudices. Let the reader judge for himself.

The disciples depart at even, putting to sea in the ship.

But, as shall recur throughout the age, the wind roared, the waters raged, and the disciples cried out for fear. To them, Jesus, asleep in the hinder part of the ship, was as good as absent. As the ship filled with the overflowing waves, terrified, they rush to wake him: 'Master, carest thou not that we perish?'

'And he arose, and rebuked the wind, and said unto the sea, Peace, be still. And the wind ceased, and there was a great calm.'

'And he said unto them, Why are ye so fearful? *how is it that ye have no faith?* And they feared exceedingly, and said one to another, What manner of man is this, that even the wind and the sea obey him?'

Master? 'Master' did they call him? Not 'Son of God'? Not 'Lord'? After the tremendous revelation of his glory over all time indicated throughout the parables? Had they seen nothing?

Why is it that ye have no faith? Even because ye believe not my word. But, when all was fulfilled, and when the Spirit was given, then they would see and know by heavenly, divine, spiritual, and mysterious revelation the reality of his person, of his work, and of his glory.

'What manner of man is this?' He is the second man, the Son from heaven, the life-giving spirit, the last Adam. He is the apostle of the new testament, he is the Sower of the word, whose it is to bestow faith, and to grant grace freely at his Father's will to the end of the age.

Their faith was to see the divine greatness of the giver, and the priceless nature of the gift. 'Thanks be unto God for his unspeakable gift.' This shall appear in the harvest, when he shall come to be admired in all them that believe.

For he shall come again, who from the womb of the morning hath the dew of his youth.

Now invisible in the heavens, to many it is still as if he were asleep in the hinder part of the ship. But he reigns above. And soon he shall appear again, consummate in glory, with the harvest raised, in the resurrection and manifestation of the sons of God, world without end. Amen.

II

The Preaching of Christ and the Gospel
Chapters 5:1 to 9:29

i. It is to the Jew first

CONCERNING the testimony of Christ to the Jews, which holds good throughout the age till the last day, the occurrences, utterances, and circumstances from the life of Jesus are rearranged by the Holy Ghost in Mark so as to form an allegorical whole, conveying the truth with telling force. This occupies the fifth and sixth chapters of Mark.

The opening phase of this apostolic ministry begins with Jesus having taken ship 'unto the other side', namely, the far side Jordan, the side of 'the country of the Gadarenes'.

This country was steeped in history reaching back to the closing days of Moses, that is, even before the time that Joshua — following Moses' death — led the people dryshod over the river into the land of inheritance promised to Abraham and his seed for ever.

Having come up from Egypt by the hand of Moses, Israel had smitten great kings and famous nations, Sihon king of the Amorites, and Og king of Bashan, bringing into subjection the lands on the east side of the river.

So it came to pass that, before Moses' decease, as the triumphant people were preparing to cross Jordan under Joshua, two and one half of the tribes of Israel drew near to petition the aged Moses.

'Now the children of Reuben and the children of Gad had a very great multitude of cattle: and when they saw the land of Jazer, and the land of Gilead, that, behold, the place was a place for cattle; the children of Gad and the children of Reuben came and spake unto Moses.' And they said, 'If we have found grace in thy sight, let this land be given unto thy servants for a possession, and bring us not over Jordan', Numbers 32:1,2, and 5.

'And Moses said unto the children of Gad and to the children of Reuben, Shall your brethren go to war, and shall ye sit here? And wherefore discourage ye the heart of the children of Israel?'

However, the men of war from the two tribes of Gad and Reuben, joined with the half tribe of Manasseh, agreed to cross over Jordan, leaving their wives, children, and cattle behind. But after the warfare which they would wage with their brethren against the inhabitants of the land, they would return.

For they had set their heart on the lush portion of the world away from the promised land on the far side Jordan, both for themselves and for their children for ever. And since they would have it, Moses gave it to them.

'For the tribe of the children of Reuben according to the house of their fathers, and the tribe of the children of Gad according to the house of their fathers, have received their inheritance; and half the tribe of Manasseh have received their inheritance: the two tribes and the half tribe have received their inheritance on this side Jordan near Jericho eastward, toward the sunrising', Numbers 34:14,15.

But what did it profit them? First the Syrians raided their pastures and cities. Then the armies of the Assyrians sacked the entire country. They deported the mass of the people, repopulated the territory with a despised foreign nation, and mixed these with the poor and pathetic remnant that was left.

Mark

Nor was this all. For above everything that had preceded, one series of conquests succeeded another, ravaging what was left of a once lush country.

Consequently the land deteriorated, the soil eroded, and the debased remnant of the ancient tribes was broken and dispossessed. From the original spreading abroad over rich pastures with great herds of cattle, the motley race that remained descended to the keeping of swine, which thing was an abomination in Israel.

'Who eat swine's flesh, and broth of abominations', Isa. 65:4. Transgressing against the law in Deuteronomy, the people that sat in darkness and in the shadow of death were ground between the upper and nether millstone of the wrath of God. And this they had for their sins, and for the sins of their fathers.

Even the names of their lands perished, and, in place, their conquerors substituted titles of their own.

Yet still God remembered Gad and the half tribe of Manasseh. He forgat not Reuben. For light had arisen, the new testament had come, and the gospel was to be preached 'to the Jew first'. But of all the Jews, the worst and lowest of the Jews, not meet to be called Jews, were those to be found on 'the other side', in the country of the Gadarenes.

The old covenant had justly excluded these mixed and polluted swineherds. They were dispossessed and disinherited. But by grace in the new testament to these first came Jesus with the gospel.

When Jesus disembarked only one man came to meet him. This man was not merely dispossessed, he was possessed; not with one, but a legion of demons.

The tormented soul—whose anguished state reflected what *all* the inhabitants of the land *ought* to have felt had they

118

been awakened to their true condition in the sight of God—came running, naked and incoherent, bloody and gashed, his broken chains and fetters swaying and jangling as he hastened to the shore.

His dwelling was in the tombs. When men would have tamed him, he plucked asunder their fetters and chains. Always, night and day, his anguished cries echoed upon the mountains, and in the tombs, where, in his torment, he cut himself with stones. Running to worship Jesus, he was so choked with demons that he was unable to use his own voice: the demons used it.

'My name is Legion: for we are many.' 'Send us not out of the country, but into the swine, that we may enter into them.' Jesus, filled with compassion for the tormented demoniac, had said, 'Come out of the man, unclean spirit'. And they came out, straightway entering into the two thousand swine, so that the whole herd ran headlong down a steep place, to be choked in the sea.

Thus the apostolic ministry of Christ in the new testament reached out not only to the lowest of the low, but of these, to the one in the most enslaved and dreadful condition. This is called Grace. It is to the Jew first. These lost sheep Jesus sought and saved. He gave gifts to the rebellious, bore the sins of many, and heard the cry of the afflicted.

Of this divine compassion the delivered man, transported with joy and thanksgiving, sitting, clothed, and in his right mind, bore witness. But now the Gadarenes, led by those who had seen what befell to him that had been possessed with the devil, and what had happened to the swine, came from all the country round about to see for themselves what it was that was done.

And they came to Jesus, and saw him that had been possessed with the devil sitting, and clothed, and in his right mind. Moreover they saw two thousand dead swine. And they were afraid. And they began to pray him to depart out of their coasts.

For the sane keepers of pigs feared a redemption that would rob them of their living, and therefore besought Jesus not for their deliverance, but for his departure. He obliged them immediately. The delivered captive begged to go with him, for he could no longer abide the sanity of his brethren.

Howbeit, Jesus suffered him not, but said unto him, Go home to thy friends, and tell them how great things the Lord hath done for thee, and hath had compassion on thee. So that despite the motley remnant of the two and a half tribes having rejected Jesus, despising the deliverance he had brought, such was the grace of God in the new testament that, on his departure, the Lord left them a witness.

As Jesus departed by ship upon the sea, immediately that obedient witness turned to go on foot throughout the land. 'And he departed, and began to publish in Decapolis how great things Jesus had done for him: and all men did marvel', Mk. 5:20.

When Jesus had passed over by ship to the other side, much people gathered unto him. This side Jordan was the true inheritance of the children of Israel, into which promised land of rest so long ago Joshua had led them dryshod over the river. However both inheritance and rest were but figures and not the reality, as the twelve tribes learned by bitter experience.

Neither the land, nor the old covenant, nor yet the works of the law, afforded any rest to Israel, neither had the daughter of Jerusalem the least peace therein. Such things awaited the coming of a better covenant, founded upon better promises, with the bringing in of a better hope by Jesus Christ, the apostle of the new covenant.

For the old covenant could not deliver from the law: indeed, it demanded the works of the law. It could not redeem from the curse: on the contrary, by it the curse sounded. Nor could the old covenant so much as face the question of sin and death: rather, it sealed the tomb of dead and guilty sinners.

Hence it is no surprise that a ruler of the synagogue—and if so a pillar of the old covenant and custodian of the law—turned in his affliction from all that which had afforded him comfort in prosperity hitherto, and fell begging at the feet of Jesus, pleading for what the law could not do: bring life. He besought Jesus for his little daughter, even at the point of death.

Now follow two incidents, that of Jairus' daughter and the woman with the issue of blood. The intertwining of these two records makes them inextricable the one from the other. If so, here lies a twofold witness of the gospel being 'to the Jew first'.

Both woman and girl are called 'Daughter', one by Jesus, the other by Jairus. The one had been brought under the curse of the law, the other brought down to the dust of death. The woman had been under the curse these twelve years, and the girl faced the king of terrors after twelve years.

Exulting over the law of sin and death, over the curse of the law and the grave, Jesus triumphed with a twofold victory: 'That I may show forth all thy praise in the gates of the daughter of Zion: I will rejoice in thy salvation', Psalm 9:14.

At the plea of her father Jairus, accompanied by a multitude, Jesus hastened to the girl lying at the point of death. But— doubtless to the extreme anguish of the father, who knew that every second counted—he was intercepted by the touch upon his clothes of a poor daughter of Abraham, bound by her plague these twelve years.

Twelve answers to the number of the covenant, and for so many years as there were tribes in Israel the woman had embodied the cursed state of those under legal bondage. But just as she had discovered by the draining of her life-blood that no help came from under the law, so she felt in herself by experience that salvation could come from none other than Jesus.

'Say ye to the daughter of Zion, Behold, thy salvation cometh; behold, his reward is with him, and his work before him.' As she but touched his garments, straightway the fountain of her blood was dried up. And she felt in her body that she was healed of that plague.

Proceeding to the little girl, Jairus' daughter, Jesus and the multitude with him are met by those bidding him go no further. They say to the father, 'Thy daughter is dead'. To Jairus, the delay had proved to be fatal.

The dead girl was but twelve years of age. This was the number of the covenant, and of the tribes of Israel. Soon the girl, raised to life, was to become the second of the two witnesses who manifested this testimony from the apostle and mediator of the new testament: To the Jew first.

Grace flowed freely in the ministration of everlasting life to the daughter of Zion brought down by the law under the sentence of death. For the legal rule had but lightly healed the wound of the daughter of God's people, saying, Peace, peace; when there was no peace. No peace so long as the rule of sin and death remained unconquered under a broken law in a failed covenant.

But righteousness and life triumphed gloriously by Jesus Christ, proclaiming 'Shake thyself from the dust'—that is, of death—'arise, and sit down, O Jerusalem: loose thyself from the bands of thy neck, O captive daughter of Zion.'

'Damsel', said Jesus to the girl descended to the dust of death, 'I say unto thee, arise. And straightway the damsel arose, and walked; for she was of the age of twelve years.' To the Jew first, seen in a twofold testimony of everlasting love to the chosen daughters of Jerusalem.

'I charge you, O daughters of Jerusalem, that ye stir not up, nor awake my love, until he please.' But now, stirred up, it pleased him to show the everlasting love with which he had espoused heavenly Jerusalem unto himself.

'For love is strong as death; jealousy is cruel as the grave: the coals thereof are coals of fire, which hath a most vehement flame. Many waters cannot quench love, neither can the floods drown it.' This is the love that came down from God out of heaven to be manifested in the person of Christ, and made known by the apostle of the new testament.

However, this witness was 'To the Jew first'.

Howbeit 'they are not all Israel, which are of Israel: neither, because they are the seed of Abraham, are they all children.' 'That is, They which are the children of the flesh, these are not the children of God: but the children of the promise are counted for the seed', Rom. 9:6-8.

Notwithstanding the Jews being of the seed of Abraham; irrespective of their springing from the stock of Israel; despite that they were Jews, faithful to the throne of David: when Jesus went with the gospel 'to the Jew first', he found few enough of the children of promise that could be counted for the seed, for all the multitudes that were born after the flesh.

Never was this more conspicuous than when in 'his own country', Mk. 6:1. The irreconcilable difference between the children of promise and the bondchildren became more evident than ever. Here appeared a divine distinction that prevailed over all, and would endure world without end.

'Is not this the carpenter?' they cried. 'And they were offended at him.' But Jesus said unto them, A prophet is not without honour, but in his own country, and among his own kin, and in his own house, Mk. 6:3,4. 'And he marvelled because of their unbelief', Mk. 6:6. And as it was with those in particular, so it happened with the Jews in general.

Nevertheless this gospel was 'to the Jew first', and thereunto was he sent. And he called unto him the twelve, and, empowering them, sent them forth into all the land, two by two. 'And they went out, and preached that men should repent', Mk. 6:12.

Thus Jesus' fame spread throughout all Israel, coming even to the ears of king Herod. At this point Mark inserts a parenthesis, Mk. 6:14-29, in which he records the influence of John the Baptist upon the king; despite this, however, Herod traps himself into beheading John. So guilty was the king's conscience, that, hearing of the famed report of Jesus and the apostles, he supposed that John the Baptist had risen from the dead.

But however much Herod had been influenced by John, it was not in favour of Christ. And if men received not John's testimony, they were hardly likely to receive him of whom he testified.

In due course the apostles returned, gathering themselves together unto Jesus, telling him of all things, both of what they had done, and what they had taught. Jesus then called them apart to a desert place to rest a while, for they were so thronged that they had no leisure so much as to eat.

And they departed into a desert place by ship privately. But the people saw, and, running afoot out of all cities, outwent them, and came together unto him. Jesus was moved with compassion towards them, because they were as sheep without a shepherd. And he began to teach them many things.

But the day being far spent, his disciples urged him to send the people away into the country round about to buy bread, for they had nothing to eat. But Jesus answered his disciples, Give ye them to eat. They replied that they had nothing save five loaves and two fishes, Mk. 6:38.

There can be no doubt that the feeding of the five thousand answers to the Jewish remnant which received the bread of life from the Lord at the hand of his apostles. The use of the number five to indicate the remnant appears again and again in the scriptures, not least in the law, where both the tabernacle, the offerings, and the excess of the firstborn over the Levites point to this conclusion.

The five wise virgins were certainly less than the full number. But the five thousand out of all Israel, from the gospel preached 'to the Jew first', would indicate even less than half the number: a remnant indeed, who, leaving all, sought the Lord in the wilderness. However the fulness of the work of God in Father, Son, and Holy Ghost, was upon them.

All this is seen in the numbers recorded. Here—as in the case of the feeding of the four thousand—the rare use of numerals to indicate spiritual truths cannot be disputed. See Mk. 8:18-21.

This is 'the remnant according to the election of grace'. Not the twelve tribes. Not even six. But a number glorifying to the God of all grace, rejecting all works, sufficient to show that 'God hath not cast away his people whom he foreknew'. Hence, 'to the Jew first.'

Under the old covenant Jehovah, invisible above, gave manna from heaven as daily bread for his people under the hand of Moses. But those who ate thereof perished. In the new covenant the Son of God on earth by his own hands miraculously multiplies bread to the remnant in the wilderness: for 'He that cometh to me shall never hunger'.

Twelve baskets of fragments remained over and above the five loaves and two fishes received by the five thousand. There was bread and to spare in the Father's house. Enough for the twelve tribes—to the Jew first—yet only proven in experience by the remnant according to the election of grace.

In this passage emphasizing the preaching of Christ and the gospel 'to the Jew first', the twelve tribes of the old covenant, reached by the twelve apostles of the new, fail of the grace of God magnified in the new testament. However the remnant according to the election of grace glorify God in his own work in the people whom he foreknew.

This is seen in the woman with the issue of blood twelve years; the damsel of the age of twelve years; Jesus calling unto him the twelve; and in the twelve baskets over. If this be not to the Jew first, What is? And if the poor remnant be not seen here, where can it be seen? But the truth is, the predestination of God is magnified in this place to his glory, whilst all the work of the flesh appears in its shame to the disgrace of Israel.

Under the old covenant Jehovah parted the waters, whereupon Moses led the people dryshod through the Red Sea. Under the new testament Jesus walks on the water, calms the sea, and stills the wind. But what else should one expect?

What else should one expect from the incarnate Son on earth, who, thousands of years before, invisible in the heavens, fed the people with daily bread, descended from above? What else from him, who, incarnate upon earth, actually walked upon the water which, invisible on high, ages aforetime he had once parted that his people should pass over dryshod?

And yet 'they were sore amazed in themselves beyond measure, and wondered.' Wondered? At what was there to wonder? There was only that to believe. But 'they considered not the miracle of the loaves: for their heart was hardened', Mk. 6:52.

Nevertheless from Christ in the gospel blessing abounded to the Jew first. 'And whithersoever he entered, into villages, or cities, or country, they laid the sick in the streets, and besought him that they might touch if it were but the border of his garment: and as many as touched him were made whole.'

However it was not the physical signs, but the spiritual things signified—that is, the seed of the word; the preaching of the gospel; the apostles' doctrine; and the mediatorship of the new testament—that brought in a better hope, founded upon better promises. It was here that the power of God stood for ever.

'For I am not ashamed of *the gospel of Christ*: for *it* is the power of God unto salvation.' And what? 'To the Jew first.' And why? Because the gospel did what the law could not do: it reached the heart.

ii. It concerns the heart

The preaching of Christ and the gospel concerns the heart. This central truth in Mark comes to light through Jesus' reply to the criticism of the Pharisees and certain scribes from Jerusalem, when they observed some of Jesus' disciples eating bread with unwashed hands, Mk. 7:1,2. The narrative next explains the basis of their faultfinding, which was grounded in the tradition of the elders, Mk. 7:3,4.

The precise wording of the protest of the Pharisees and scribes to Jesus follows: 'Why walk not thy disciples according to the tradition of the elders, but eat bread with unwashen hands?', Mk. 7:5.

Jesus responds with a cutting denunciation against their substitution of the traditions of men for the word of God, a practice which had grown increasingly until it filled all Jewry. 'Well hath Esaias prophesied of you hypocrites, as it is written, This people honoureth me with their lips, but their heart is far from me. Howbeit in vain do they worship me, teaching for doctrines the commandments of men', Mk. 7:6,7.

By these words Jesus condemns the leaders, from first to last, as nothing but hypocrites. He proceeds to include all the people under them. He dismisses their lip-service as worthless because their inward hearts told another tale. There you have it: the heart.

'For the LORD seeth not as man seeth; for man looketh on the outward appearance, but the LORD looketh on the heart', I Samuel 16:7. For all their fair words and fervent speeches, their hearts gave the lie to their lips. Jesus calls this vanity false worship: 'Howbeit in vain do they worship me', Mk. 7:7.

Here was a people professing to worship in words, appearances, and forms, as had their fathers before them. Over the generations they had developed numerous customs contrary to the word of God. These customs were called 'the traditions of the elders'.

But Jesus exposed their traditions, teaching that worship stood neither in words, confessions, forms, nor in ceremonies. In fact worship stood not in anything that man could do. Hands, lips, postures, gestures, acts, performances: these were things that man could do. What man could not do pertained to the heart.

Jesus' words astonished the people, all of whom thereupon he called unto him, admonishing them not only to hearken, but to understand.

This is the central teaching: central to Mark; central to the truth. 'There is nothing from without a man, that entering into him can defile him: but the things which come out of him, those are they that defile the man. If any man have ears to hear, let him hear', Mk. 7:15,16.

This is at the hub of Jesus' teaching in Mark. It is not as if he were expounding the doctrine of the gospel in and of itself.

He is revealing that to which the doctrine is directed; that in which the gospel seed is planted. It is not the seed of the word of which he is speaking: he speaks of the *only ground in which that seed, once sown, bears enduring fruit.* He speaks of the heart.

This is central to Jesus' teaching in Mark. He is not expounding the apostolic doctrine of Christ: he is teaching *where that doctrine must be received.* It is not the seed of the word that he is opening: it is *the place where that seed must be sown.* Agreeable to the parable, the seed was one thing: the ground was another. Here, Jesus shows the ground. He that hath ears to hear, let him hear.

After these words Jesus entered into the house from the people, to teach his disciples within. There they asked him about the parable, Mk. 7:17.

He responded, Are ye so without understanding also? Evidently they were, for it was true that neither those without nor those within yet appeared to understand the interior illumination of God to the heart. This commenced with a prior work of revelation, in which the inner man—otherwise in darkness—was brought into the light.

Then, and not till then, the soul was enlightened as to its true condition, and made to feel by experience its defilement and alienation from God. This preparatory work was the beginning of the salvation of God in the hidden man of the heart.

'For from within, out of the heart of men, proceed evil thoughts, adulteries, fornications, murders, thefts, covetousness, wickedness, deceit, lasciviousness, an evil eye, blasphemy, pride, foolishness: all these evil things come from within'—Jesus does not refer to these things breaking out, or appearing externally: here they are inward—'and defile the man', Mk. 7:21-23.

When God makes manifest this depraved mass of unmitigated evil seething within the heart, the forms of religion are

129

eschewed. Of what use then are works, performances, or the traditions of the elders teaching a system of words, creeds, prayers, and observances, to be acceptable with God?

Such a soul knows that it can *never* be acceptable with God in and of itself. 'From the sole of the foot even unto the head there is no soundness in it; but wounds, and bruises, and putrifying sores', Isa. 1:6.

Then how deceived are those who—in common with all mankind—possess such a state within, yet, whitewashing the exterior, draw near to God with their lips, whilst their heart is far from him?

On the contrary the enlightened soul cries, 'The heart of the sons of men is full of evil', Ecc. 9:3. 'The heart is deceitful above all things, and desperately wicked: who can know it?', Jer. 17:9. The convicted sinner knows it, and hence gives forth the cry, 'Create in me a clean heart, O God; and renew a right spirit within me', Ps. 51:10.

This experimental discovery of the total inward depravity common to all men is the beginning of the work of God in the soul: it is in fact the preparation of the good ground.

When this work is completed, God declares: 'A new heart also will I give you, and a new spirit will I put within you: and I will take away the stony heart out of your flesh, and I will give you an heart of flesh', Ezek. 36:26.

To effect such a work the Spirit of God takes his sword and thrusts it right into the depths of the heart, cutting to right and left, till all lies exposed.

'For the word of God is quick, and powerful, and sharper than any twoedged sword, piercing even to the dividing asunder of soul and spirit, and of the joints and marrow, and is a discerner of the thoughts and intents of the heart', Heb. 4:12.

Now all the religion of man, the tradition of the elders, and the works of the flesh are refused. Every form of patching up the outward man with a show of religion is abominated. All offers of whitewash for the exterior appearances are detested.

Nothing, but nothing, save the work of God in giving eternal life will do for the convicted soul. And this the Sower does by dropping the living and heavenly seed into the prepared ground.

God brought the man to a sight of his disease: only God can bring him to the experience of the cure.

'For he is not a Jew, which is one outwardly; neither is that circumcision, which is outward in the flesh: but he is a Jew, which is one inwardly; and circumcision is that of the heart, in the spirit, and not in the letter; whose praise is not of men, but of God', Rom. 2:28,29.

For the gospel of Christ concerns the heart, which is prepared of God to receive both Christ and gospel by the divine revelation of the true state of the inner man. This state the soul freely owns. Hence the cry arises to God, 'A broken and a contrite heart, O God, thou wilt not despise', Ps. 51:17.

Now the ground is prepared, and the heavenly Sower draws near, broadcasting the seed. The result is called 'the seed sown in good ground'. This is central to Jesus' teaching in Mark.

Further, the preaching of Christ and the gospel, though to the Jew first, withal concerning the heart, is also to the Gentile. Observe this.

iii. It is to the Gentile also

For God is not the God of the Jews only, but of the Gentiles also. 'Seeing it is one God, which shall justify the circumcision by faith, and uncircumcision through faith', Rom. 3:30.

131

Although justification by faith is a truth the full revelation of which awaited the consummation of the death, resurrection, and ascension of Christ, with the consequent descent of the Holy Ghost, still, justification was ever inherent in the heavenly seed of the word.

The preparation of the good ground to receive that seed pertained to the Gentiles also, and this the next section of Mark declares in a figure.

The time of the Gentiles was not yet come, but Christ had come with the gospel to the Jews, and just as by earthly and physical signs and wonders he showed forth that heavenly and spiritual salvation which should abide for ever, so by figure and allegory he showed also that the gospel was yet to go forth to the Gentile nations.

This would occur when Christ, having ascended, the Spirit being given, next called out a people who were once not a people. For he would bring forth judgment to the Gentiles, and would fulfil the ancient hope of the Isles that waited for his law.

Then should come to pass the saying which was written, 'For this cause I will confess to thee among the Gentiles, and sing unto thy name.' And again he saith, 'Rejoice, ye Gentiles, with his people.' Once more: 'Praise the Lord, all ye Gentiles; and laud him, all ye people.'

Of this the prophet Esaias foretold, saying, 'In that day there shall be a root of Jesse, and he that shall rise to reign over the Gentiles; in him shall the Gentiles trust.' The fulfilment of this does not appear at this point in Mark, for he that should rise to reign over the Gentiles was not yet risen. Indeed, he had not yet been put to death.

Esaias' prophecy therefore finds its fulfilment after the cross, and beyond the resurrection, when Christ should rise and ascend into heaven, sending forth the Holy Ghost, thence-forth to reign over the Gentiles from the heavenly glory.

However, Mark does *prefigure* the truth of this—spiritual—coming of Christ and the gospel to the Gentiles in the passage beginning at chapter 7:24 and concluding with chapter 8:9.

Leaving the place where he had shown that the gospel was to the Jew first, withal concerning the heart, Jesus' testimony of that which was to come to the Gentiles also now commences: 'And from thence he arose, and went into the borders of Tyre and Sidon.' Now, Tyre and Sidon were Gentile cities well to the north of the uttermost borders of Galilee.

There he entered into a house, and would have no man know it, but he could not be hid. For a certain woman, whose young daughter had an unclean spirit, heard of him, and came and fell at his feet.

Here is one taught of God in a broken heart to come to the Saviour. And here is the bondage of mankind to the world, the flesh, and the devil, all brought home by tragedy, and set forth in a figure.

Moreover here it is evident that the time had not yet come. No, but the figure of that time was come, and the desperate woman sought to grasp at the opportunity which it brought. 'But Jesus said unto her, Let the children first be filled: for it is not meet to take the children's bread, and to cast it unto the dogs', Mk. 7:27.

She takes no offence; her contrite heart is beyond offence; no expression is too low for her to make any objection: only, let him grant her his salvation.

'Yes, Lord'—mark that: Lord—'yet the dogs under the table eat of the children's crumbs.' Here is preparatory work in evidence, and on its heels salvation comes to her house: 'The devil is gone out of thy daughter', Mk. 7:29.

'And again, departing from the coasts of Tyre and Sidon, he came unto the sea of Galilee, through the midst of the coasts of Decapolis', Mk. 7:31. Decapolis, a Gentile territory, lay on the far side Jordan, with its western boundary fetching a compass about the far shore of the sea of Galilee.

'And they bring unto him one that was deaf, and had an impediment in his speech; and they beseech him to put his hand upon him', Mk. 7:32.

Jesus took aside the man who could neither hear nor speak, and put his fingers into his ears, and spat, and touched his tongue. Then, looking up to heaven, he breathed a sigh, saying in Hebrew, Ephphatha, that is, Be opened.

Here was the Gentile who heard nothing from God or man; who could articulate neither to his Creator nor his fellows. And there was the God of the Gentiles also, whose fingers formed man from the dust of the ground in the beginning, and who breathed into man the breath of life at the first. Now God manifest in the flesh brings in a new creation at the last, here seen in a figure.

In himself he makes of twain—Jew and Gentile—one new man, so making peace. This is prefigured in Mark by his going to the Gentiles. Directly or indirectly the narrative has referred to Tyre, Sidon, Syria, Phoenicia, Greece, the nations, and Decapolis. In a word, 'To the Gentiles also'.

But for all this, the time had not yet come: however there was given a figure, a sign to the Gentile multitude 'being very great'. But a sign which should find fulfilment after Jesus' death and resurrection on the third day. This is the feeding of the four thousand, Mk. 8:1-9.

If in the figure, the multitude 'have now been with me three days', and the feeding of the four thousand set forth Christ's reign after death from the glory, then that multitude signified those who had died with him.

More. They prefigure those who were buried together with Christ, and who were risen with him the third day to newness of life, henceforth to be sustained with the heavenly bread of life from the glory. Thus he should rise to reign over the Gentiles.

He should rise to reign over the Gentiles, delivering them from the wilderness of this world, ministering heavenly sustenance spiritually conveyed on earth, guiding them as pilgrims and strangers to the glory of the world to come.

There is perfect provision for the Gentiles also: seven loaves. Seven is the number of perfection, as it appears so clearly in holy writ, where the relatively rare cases of the figurative use of numerals becomes evident from the distinctive nature of the context.

Here in the sign, this perfect provision extends to the four corners of the earth, that is, the nations from all quarters.

Such an abundance of grace is all of God: perfect provision assured and administered by Father, Son, and Holy Ghost, secure to all the seed. This is seen in the number fed, four multiplied by ten three times over. Withal, seven baskets over.

Hence the complete work of God, provided to perfection, sustains the redeemed of the Lord throughout this earthly pilgrimage, till the world to come shall have come to pass, and, being raised in his likeness, they shall see him as he is. Thus, to the Gentiles also.

Next Mark brings before us the truth that the preaching of Christ and the gospel is without respect of persons.

iv. It is without respect of persons

And why not? For there had been neither criticism, opposition, nor persecution from the Gentiles, who cried, astonished beyond measure, 'He hath done all things well: he maketh both the deaf to hear, and the dumb to speak.'

After the feeding of the four thousand 'Straightway he entered into a ship with his disciples, and came into the parts of Dalmanutha', Mk. 8:10. This was in the coasts of Magdala, Mt. 15:39, where Jews of a sort resided, dwelling in the uttermost parts of Israel, no more than the borders.

Immediately the Pharisees came forth. In which case they had been waiting. They could not go over to the lands of the Gentiles, that would be too unclean; howbeit the despised outskirts of 'Galilee of the Gentiles' were just bearable to suffer till Jesus returned.

But why wait? Why come forth? To say, 'He hath done all things well'? No; to criticize, tempt, and persecute. 'And the Pharisees came forth, and began to question with him, seeking of him a sign from heaven, tempting him', Mk. 8:11.

These were the standard-bearers of doctrine, the champions of the truth, the custodians of orthodoxy. But of what spirit were they, who *tempted* Jesus to show a sign *from heaven*? They were of the same spirit as the one who said 'Cast thyself down' —from the pinnacle of the temple—'for it is written, He shall give his angels charge concerning thee.'

They were of the spirit of their father the devil, but blind to it, being infatuated with their own righteousness, enamoured of their self-justification, and obsessed with the letter of scripture. Which scripture both their spirit and life denied.

But the root lay in birth. When Jesus had sighed deeply in his spirit, he said, 'There shall no sign be given unto this generation', Mk. 8:12. A serpent's seed; sons of disobedience; children of wrath: the succession of birth, the line of 'this' generation, went back to the first man Adam. For 'by one man sin entered into the world.'

'Generation' answers to succession. And religion, the worse for being orthodox, provides the maximum aggravation to such a seed. Nothing but regeneration in a new heart, and mortification in the denial of the old, can counter 'this generation'.

There are but two generations: The children of God by the glory of Christ; and the children of the devil by the fall of man. 'We know that we are of God, and the whole world lieth in wickedness', I Jn. 5:19.

'Little children, let no man deceive you: he that doeth righteousness is righteous, even as he is righteous. He that committeth sin is of the devil; for the devil sinneth from the beginning', I Jn. 3:7,8. 'In this the children of God are manifest, and the children of the devil', I Jn. 3:10. There are no other. No generations exist other than these.

Neither can scripture, orthodoxy, worship, reformation, or anything that man can do, or men do for man, deliver from the old. There is no respect of persons. There must be a new creation, wrought in the heart by the mediator and apostle of the new testament. Nothing less brings to the birth, or brings to the light, the generation of God's children.

God has no respect to whatsoever is attained after the flesh, or wrought by the will of man, or stands in the blood of ancient lineage. The religion of 'this generation' avails nothing. There is no respect of persons with God. 'And he left them, and entering into the ship again departed to the other side.' The Gentile side.

A sign from heaven? Yet no more than two signs on earth were enough for the Gentiles. Then what of the signs in Israel?

The lame walk; the deaf hear; the dumb speak; the lepers are cleansed; the blind see; the sick are healed; the devils are cast out; and the dead are raised to life again. And, in Israel, how many times over and over again?

As to that generation, Seeing they saw, but did not perceive; hearing they heard, but did not understand; lest at any time they should be converted, and their sins should be forgiven them, Mk. 4:12.

Sign? But they had seen; they had heard. Twelve baskets of fragments had been gathered after the five thousand—figure of the remnant of Israel—had been fed. And was this not enough and to spare for the twelve tribes? And what greater sign from heaven, than bread from heaven?

And was it not—this excess of the twelve baskets—without respect of persons? Who among the seed of Jacob was excluded? But those who sought a sign had excluded themselves.

What greater sign from heaven than that which had been given? And had they not heard—since they were waiting for him on their side of the sea—of the like sign in the feeding of the four thousand? And was not perfect provision for the Gentiles sign enough, in excess over and above the four thousand who were fed? And they seek a sign from heaven?

But the disciples themselves were likewise obtuse. Warned by Jesus of the leaven of the Pharisees and of Herod, they thought, as they crossed the sea, that this was because they had no bread. But, Mk. 8:17, it was perception which they lacked; it was understanding that was missing.

'Have ye your heart yet hardened? Having eyes, see ye not? and having ears, hear ye not? and do ye not remember? When I brake the five loaves among five thousand, how many baskets full of fragments took ye up? They say unto him, Twelve. And when the seven among four thousand, how many baskets full of fragments took ye up? And they said, Seven', Mk. 8:18-20.

And if any will say to me that the feeding of the five thousand and of the four thousand are not places for the spiritual and symbolic use of numbers, let them apply to themselves the six questions of Mk. 8:17,18.

Finally, 'He said unto them, How is it that ye do not understand?', Mk. 8:21. These words also are without respect of persons.

'And he cometh to Bethsaida; and they bring a blind man unto him, and besought him to touch him.' They may bring the blind man, but it was they themselves who were blind, for, having eyes, they saw not.

'Woe unto thee, Bethsaida! for if the mighty works, which were done in you, had been done in Tyre and Sidon, they would have repented long ago in sackcloth and ashes', Mt. 11:21.

However the mediator and apostle of the covenant will not be restricted by the unbelief and hardness of heart of the religious, who, having eyes, see not. 'And he took the blind man by the hand, and led him out of the town.' He separated the man in whom he was to show forth his power and glory in the new testament, leaving them behind in their congregation.

Alone, he spat upon the blind man's eyes, and put his hands upon him, and asked him if he saw ought.

And the man looked up, and said, I see men as trees, walking. This restored to the first creation, but it was rooted in the earth, and destined for the dust from whence it came. But he saw that. Which is what the Jews could not see.

However another covenant, a new creation, that which comes down from God out of heaven was at hand. Restoration of the old was not enough, nor did it answer to God's eternal purpose. But the apostle of the new testament answered to God's eternal purpose.

When the moisture in the breath from the mouth of the Creator, and the hands of him who made all things at the beginning, restored the blind man's sight, *the man* looked up. But when the mediator and apostle of the new testament brought in a new creation from the old, laying on hands *again*, *he made* the man look up. If so, to heaven.

From such a view, all was clear, and restoration was to the image of Christ. See Mk. 8:22-26.

Only from the Father in heaven comes the true—the spiritual and interior—knowledge of Christ, and it comes by revelation. 'Thou art the Christ.' But darkness covers the earth, and the veil is upon the face of all people, and—whether searching the scriptures or not—those who look at the earth, who are earthy, blunder in confusion.

'And he charged them that they should tell no man of him', Mk. 8:30. 'And he began to teach them, that the Son of man must suffer many things, and be rejected of the elders, and of the chief priests, and scribes, and be killed, and after three days rise again. And he spake that saying openly. And Peter took him, and began to rebuke him', Mk. 8:31,32.

Rebuke him? But Jesus being killed, and after three days rising again, laid the only foundation for God righteously to forgive sins, and justly to deliver from the law and its curse. There was no other basis on which the mediator could establish the new testament.

And should Peter rebuke him for submitting to that suffering pathway which alone could make effectual all that he came into the world to achieve for God and man?

Peter rebuked him for submitting to those who sought to destroy him. Because Peter felt that Jesus had the power in his life to establish an earthly kingdom for God in Israel. But that power given to Jesus was to bring in a heavenly kingdom in the world to come. It was for the inheritance in the everlasting glory. If so, past death, beyond time, and when this world was no more.

When Jesus had turned about and looked on his disciples, he rebuked Peter, saying, Get thee behind me, Satan: for thou savourest not the things that be of God, but the things that be of men, Mk. 8:33. And where is respect of persons in that? There is no respect of persons in that.

The former were Jesus' words, and they were of God. The latter were Peter's words, and they were of Satan. Christ and his gospel were not for this present world, but for deliverance from it, to bring in the world to come. Satan and his false gospel were for this present world, bringing in for this age a man-pleasing religion to deceive the whole earth.

Therefore Jesus saith, 'Whosoever will come after me, let him deny himself, and take up his cross, and follow me.' That is, as a pilgrim and stranger, through suffering and death, to everlasting glory. 'For whosoever will save his life shall lose it; but whosoever shall lose his life for my sake and the gospel's, the same shall save it', Mk. 8:35.

'For what shall it profit a man, if he shall gain the whole world, and lose his own soul?' Better to lose the world, and save his soul. Better to deny oneself, take up the cross, and follow Christ and the gospel. The path may lead through suffering and death, but it surely brings to everlasting glory.

'Whosoever therefore shall be ashamed of me and of my words in this adulterous and sinful generation; of him also shall the Son of man be ashamed, when he cometh in the glory of his Father with the holy angels', Mk. 8:38. This applied just as much to Peter; indeed it expanded Jesus' cutting rebuke to Peter. For there is no respect of persons with God.

Nor would the coming of the kingdom tarry: there were those standing there, who would not taste of death, till they had seen the kingdom of God come with power. Among these was the chastened and penitent Peter, who was present when suddenly there came from heaven a sound of a rushing mighty wind, which filled the house where they were sitting.

Peter was present when there appeared unto them cloven tongues like as of fire, and it sat upon each of them. And they were all filled with the Holy Ghost, and began to speak with other tongues, as the Spirit gave them utterance.

He was there: because he submitted; he denied himself; he took up his cross; he received chastisement: hence he saw—he experienced—the kingdom of God come with power, Mk. 9:1.

Finally, chapter 9:1-29, the record in Mark leads to the clear impression from his doctrine concerning the preaching of Christ and the gospel that it is both heavenly and glorious, in a word, it follows the ascension.

v. It is from the glory

This passage opens with a visionary revelation which foreshadowed the glorious appearance of Christ following the resurrection and after the ascension. This is called the transfiguration, a vision given to three witnesses only, taken apart even from the twelve.

The vision was not to be made known till after the resurrection. Nevertheless this revelation shows how the apostle of the covenant will appear in the administration of the new testament from the glory, to this present day, and even to the end of the age.

This reveals to a demonstration that the preaching of Christ and the gospel is from the glory. From thence comes the ministration of the Spirit. If so, Christ *himself* administers the new testament by that Spirit and from the glory. Otherwise it is not the ministry of the new testament. It is just men or organizations with a dead book.

Everything in the passage confirms the truth that Christ ministers the new testament from the glory, and that this is how he appears in glory from the ascension.

Here is 'the glorious gospel of Christ', II Cor. 4:4. It is the glory of God shining in the face of Jesus Christ, II Cor. 4:6. It is the ministration of righteousness that exceeds in glory, II Cor. 3:9. It is the beholding the glory of the Lord, II Cor. 3:18. That is what the vision on the mount of transfiguration reveals beforehand.

Mark records that Jesus took Peter, James, and John, 'and leadeth them up into an high mountain apart by themselves: and he was transfigured before them', Mk. 9:2.

This ascent began 'after six days'. If so, on the seventh day. Nevertheless, the seventh day was not the day of the transfiguration. It was the day of the ascent. '*After* six days' Jesus 'leadeth them up into an high mountain.'

But how is it determined that the ascent took up a whole day, that is, the seventh day? Because immediately *following* the ascension Luke states, 'And it came to pass, that on the *next* day, *when* they were come down', Lk. 9:37.

If on the *next* day—after the day of transfiguration—they came down, then that day was occupied with making the descent. And if the descent took up that day, it is hardly likely that the more arduous ascent would have taken less time. Then if—as Mark tells us—they began the ascent *after* six days, the day of their ascending must have been the seventh day.

143

It follows that the transfiguration was on the first day. This is confirmed by Luke when he embraces the whole period by saying that it was 'About an eight days', Lk. 9:28.

After six days they began their ascent, that is, on the seventh day. The day following, the first day, Jesus was transfigured before them. The next day they made their descent. For 'it came to pass, on the next day, when they were come down', Lk. 9:37. In all, 'about an eight days', Lk. 9:28.

Does this matter? Yes, it matters that the transfiguration was on the first day of the week, because that was the day of the resurrection, and the vision requires the parallel in time. 'Very early in the morning the first day of the week', Mk. 16:2. This is the glorious resurrection day, to which the vision of Christ in his glory properly belongs.

Hence in the vision of that coming glory, 'he was transfigured before them'. That is, he was transformed, 'made to appear in another form', namely, the form in which his glory should appear from the resurrection and in the ascension. This is the form in which he should minister the new testament from the other side of death, from his glorious appearing in the heavens.

He was transfigured on the first day, the resurrection day, and so he admonishes them: 'As they came down from the mountain, he charged them that they should tell no man what things they had seen, *till the Son of man were risen from the dead*', Mk. 9:9. Therefore the vision pertains to the resurrection and the glory. And the day was that day on which he should rise from the dead.

This glorious ministry of the mediator and apostle of the new testament is to a separated company. It is to the *ecclesia*, brought by the divine inworking of the Father from heaven into the apostles' fellowship. 'And truly our fellowship is with the Father, and with his Son Jesus Christ', I Jn. 1:3.

This fellowship separates from the world, and from earthly religion, as it is written, 'And of the rest durst no man join himself to them', Acts 5:13. Within this separated company the glory shone from heaven. Of this, Jesus taking Peter, James, and John *apart*, is significant. And it is 'apart *by themselves*'.

Likewise he was transfigured 'before them'. Again, 'There appeared *unto them* Moses and Elias.' These things are within the sanctuary. They belong to the separated people of God. They cannot be seen from without.

The high mountain signifies the new testament, just as mount Sinai had indicated the old. 'Which things are an allegory: for these are the two covenants; the one from the mount Sinai, which gendereth to bondage.' This 'answereth to Jerusalem which now is, and is in bondage with her children', Gal. 4:24,25.

'But Jerusalem which is above is free, which is the mother of us all', Gal. 4:26. And, 'Ye are come unto mount Sion, and unto the city of the living God, the heavenly Jerusalem', Heb. 12:22.

This appears in another vision: 'I looked, and, lo, a Lamb stood on the mount Sion, and with him an hundred forty and four thousand, having his Father's name written in their foreheads', Rev. 14:1. But his Father's name is disclosed only in the new testament, and only under the ministry of the Son: 'I have declared unto *them* thy name', Jn. 17:26.

Thus God declares, 'Yet have I set my king upon my holy hill of Zion', Ps. 2:6. This mount Zion, which is the new testament, heavenly Jerusalem, Jerusalem above, called God's holy hill, to which the resurrection and ascension of Christ pertain, and upon which God—who raised him from the dead—set him in heavenly glory, is shown in a figure beforehand by the 'high mountain' of the transfiguration.

From thence Christ mediates and declares the new testament, as it is written, 'Sit thou at my right hand, until I make thine enemies thy footstool'. This is the ascension, Ps. 110:1.

Again, 'The LORD shall send the rod of thy strength out of Zion.' Here Christ is ascended to heavenly mount Zion, having entered into his glory, from thence to administer the new testament in the power and strength of the Holy Ghost, Ps. 110:2. All this the mount of transfiguration typified. If not, why go up into the mount? why be transfigured before them?

But Peter settles the matter, interpreting the transfiguration, II Pet. 1:16-18. 'We were eyewitnesses of his majesty', he declares. But when? Evidently before Christ took up his glorious reign on high. Then when? 'When we made known unto you the power and coming of our Lord Jesus Christ.'

But when was Peter eyewitness of the power and coming of our Lord Jesus Christ? For Peter here affirms Jesus' name from the glory.

'Lord Jesus Christ' is Jesus' title commencing from the glorious heavenly ascension. Peter declares that he was an eyewitness of that: 'When there came such a voice to him from the excellent glory, This is my beloved Son, in whom I am well pleased', II Pet. 1:17.

But this voice came at Jesus' baptism, of which John the Baptist was eyewitness, not Peter and the apostles. Then how does Peter say that they were eyewitnesses, and heard that voice?

'And this voice which came from heaven *we* heard'—that is, *also* heard, not on the same occasion, but nevertheless the same voice—'when we were with him in the holy mount', II Pet. 1:18.

It was on that *second* occasion that Peter was an eyewitness, actually hearing the same voice. *That* was when 'we were

146

eyewitnesses of his majesty', Peter prophetically declaring the ascended title of 'Lord Jesus Christ' to describe the majesty of the transfiguration.

From which it follows by apostolic interpretation that the transfiguration, though given during the days of his flesh, provided a vision of the glorious appearing of Christ risen from the dead and ascended into heaven.

And this must follow, since from thence comes the voice of him that speaketh from heaven, mediating the new testament by the strength and power of the Spirit 'sent forth out of Zion' to glorify him in the midst of the assembly.

Unlike Matthew and Luke, Mark does not mention the transfiguration of the Lord's countenance. However he has more to say than either concerning his raiment. This is what covers the body. Mark adds to the record that his raiment became shining, exceeding white as snow, and that this was 'so as no fuller on earth can white them', Mk. 9:3.

But who were the fullers on earth? 'And there appeared unto them Elias with Moses: and they were talking with Jesus', Mk. 9:4.

Moses could indeed bring in an outward rectitude. To this Saul of Tarsus laid claim: 'Touching the righteousness which is in the law, blameless', Phil. 3:6. But blameless before man only. What? Blameless, and a soul as dark as night? What? Blameless, and persecute Christ and his saints? What? Blameless, with an uncircumcised heart filled with enmity? All such righteousnesses are but filthy rags, Isa. 64:6.

Elias also was a fuller: he had come — as had Moses before him — and found few enough who would attempt to whiten their garments under his prescription. He restoreth all things: yes, but did it last? No it did not, and him they slew.

But the righteousness of God which is by faith of Jesus Christ, administered from the glory of heaven, provided other garments. The divine fuller brought in that which exceeded anything conceivable on earth, and brought it in by another on behalf of the elect, even by Jesus Christ.

Other fullers, fullers on earth, directed men to clean their own garments. But Christ by the gospel provides different raiment altogether, so as no fuller on earth can white them.

When this is done by grace through faith in the glorious gospel of the blessed God, there is no need of earthly fullers. 'This is my beloved Son: hear him.' 'And suddenly, when they had looked round about, they saw no man any more, save Jesus only with themselves', Mk. 9:8.

But if in a vision Jesus appeared as glorified above, then in a like figure there follows a revelation of all that is found below. Jesus descended to find questioning scribes; unbelieving apostles; perplexed disciples; amazed crowds; a faithless generation; a desperately afflicted father; and a pitifully possessed son. That is what lies below. Yet to it the glorified Son condescended and yet condescends.

The father cried, 'Master, I have brought unto thee my son, which hath a dumb spirit; and wheresoever he taketh him, he teareth him: and he foameth, and gnasheth with his teeth, and pineth away: and I spake to thy disciples that they should cast him out; and they could not.'

'He answereth him, and saith, O faithless generation, how long shall I be with you? how long shall I suffer you? bring him unto me', Mk. 9:17-19.

Observe that it is a question of a generation: 'O faithless generation.' Ultimately a generation runs back to the first man. The progenitor. That man was the genesis. He generated the issue. He was the father of it all. What is seen here is that the generation had not at all evolved for the better. Rather it had degenerated to the worst.

And so the distraught father found to his cost: 'Ofttimes it hath cast him into the fire, and into the waters, to destroy him.' This had not happened to the father. Although what had occurred to the father was tragedy enough. But what had possessed the son was worse beyond measure.

The context of father and son; the dreadful state of the son having come upon him 'of a child', Mk. 9:21; the child having been *born* in this state; the contextual use of the word 'generation': all point to this issue expressing the condition of mankind in the world from birth.

'Behold, I was shapen in iniquity; and in sin did my mother conceive me', Ps. 51:5. 'The wicked are estranged from the womb'—that is before birth—'they go astray as soon as they be born, speaking lies'—that is from birth, Ps. 58:3.

'By one man sin entered into the world', Paul teaches us, Rom. 5:12, adding, 'By one man's disobedience many were made sinners', Rom. 5:19. The apostle refers to the generation of mankind not only as being 'dead in trespasses and sins', Eph. 2:1, but also as walking 'according to the course of this world'.

Moreover, though not taken so violently, or even obviously at all—as was the child with the dumb spirit—still it is true of the whole world, of mankind, that all are governed 'according to the prince of the power of the air, the *spirit* that *now worketh* in the children of disobedience', Eph. 2:2.

It was this that the Son of God found when he came into the world, and found to be universal. And it is this that Christ finds as he descends from the holy mount in the Spirit and with the gospel. This is depicted in the figure. Likewise the *true*, but largely *undiscovered* condition of the generation of mankind appears in the child possessed of the foul spirit.

In desperation, answering Jesus' words, 'If thou canst believe, all things are possible to him that believeth', straightway the agonized father of the child cried out with tears, 'Lord, I believe; help thou mine unbelief'. And believe in Christ he did: anguish had wrought the work of a broken and contrite spirit. At first it was 'Master', Mk. 9:17; but now it is 'Lord', Mk. 9:24.

Jesus rebuked the foul spirit, saying unto him, Thou dumb and deaf spirit, I charge thee, come out of him, and enter no more into him. And the spirit cried, and rent him sore, and came out of him: and he was as one dead; insomuch that many said, He is dead. But Jesus took him by the hand, and lifted him up; and he arose. Mk. 9:25-27.

And when he was come into the house, his disciples asked him privately, Why could not we cast him out? Now, these disciples were those left below when Jesus took Peter, James, and John with him up into the high mountain apart by themselves.

Peter, James, and John beheld his glory. They saw his radiant appearance, transfigured, as he should be manifest by revelation when ministering the new testament by the Spirit from the glory of heaven after his ascension.

But those left below did not see this: they had no such exalted views of Christ. To them he answers, This kind can come forth by nothing, but by prayer and fasting. But not anybody's prayer and fasting. After all, the disciples of John and of the Pharisees used to fast, Mk. 2:18, but this had no effect at all.

Those who had ascended into the hill of the Lord, however, who had seen the heavenly vision, who beheld his glory, to whom the Father had revealed the Son, these were in the secret.

Three days they had been with him, and, it would appear, fasting. But it was *his* prayer and fasting, *his* living and dying, *his* rising and ascending, which those who were with him in the holy mount observed, attended, and trusted.

All authority was *his*. At *his* command every unclean spirit must obey. He who was from above all, descended beneath all, and rose again over all, having power over all flesh, to give eternal life to as many as the Father gave to him.

God had anointed him with the Holy Ghost and with power, who went about doing good, and healing all that were oppressed of the devil; for God was with him. And he was with God: to him he prayed, for him he fasted, and through him he gave himself. And God raised him to glory. 'Lord, to whom else shall we go? *thou* hast the words of eternal life.'

These words of eternal life he speaks from heaven, by the Spirit on earth, even to this day. Radiant in light unapproachable, high over all, his word is irresistible.

Then if the preaching of Christ and the gospel be from the glory, it follows also that by such things he condescends to the poor and afflicted, the despised and outcast, the bound and imprisoned, to give deliverance upon the earth below, and salvation from the prince of the power of the air, the spirit which now worketh in the children of disobedience.

This passage now brings to a conclusion the second great division in the marvellous revelation of the beginning of the gospel of Jesus Christ, the Son of God, called, The Gospel according to Mark.

III

The Distinction of Christ and the Gospel
Chapters 9:30 to 13

i. It is not for this world's society

THIS passage—as everything that is in common between its
incidents, discourses, and their arrangement in sequence
demonstrates—teaches that the ministry of Christ in the new
testament is not with a view to this world, but for that which
is to come. It is given in this world, but it is neither of it nor
for it. Indeed, this world is regarded as judged already.

Hence they that are Christ's are 'crucified unto the world,
and the world unto them'. They are not of the world: he has
chosen them out of the world. They see clearly that all that is
in the world, the lust of the flesh, the lust of the eyes, and the
pride of life, is not of the Father, but is of the world. And the
world passeth away, and the lust thereof, but he that doeth
the will of God abideth for ever.

Wherefore they love not the world, neither the things that
are of the world, knowing that if any man love the world, the
love of the Father is not in him. They feel, and feel strongly,
that friendship with the world is enmity against God. 'My
kingdom is not of this world', said Jesus: hence he prayed to
the Father concerning those who are of that kingdom, saying,
'They are not of the world, even as I am not of the world'.

To the spiritual the world is regarded as an entity, an entire
system, an economy or arrangement, summed up in the mystical

concept of 'Babylon'. To this system Christ's apostolic ministry of the new testament yields nothing. Neither does such a system yield anything to that ministry, because the world is based on entirely different and contrary principles, deliverance from which is of the essence in the gospel.

Just as the children of Israel were called out of Egypt to journey through the wilderness to the promised land, so the children of God are called in spirit to be separate from this world, passing the time of their sojourning here in fear. As pilgrims and strangers on the earth, they look for a better resurrection, thence to inherit the glory of the kingdom prepared for them from the foundation of the world.

This spiritual reality is equally true of the old testament saints: 'These all died in faith, not having received the promises, but having seen them afar off, and were persuaded of them, and embraced them, and confessed that they were strangers and pilgrims on the earth.'

'But now they desire a better country, that is, an heavenly: wherefore God is not ashamed to be called their God: for he hath prepared for them a city.' God was *their* God. As to the god of *this* world, the entire world, Paul reveals that the god of this world is Satan, II Cor. 4:4.

However, pilgrims and strangers, begotten through the promise of God in the gospel, are not merely separate from the world in an outward way: a spiritual, new, and inward character has been wrought in them which makes them entirely different. They are different *in their nature* from the world. That is what the passage in Mk. 9:30 to 10:52 shows. There is a distinction, and it is a distinction in nature.

Moreover, wholly in contrast with this present world, there is a coming sphere, with a heavenly arrangement, a new creation, a divine economy. This is the world to come, whereof we speak. It is to *this* that the new testament pertains.

The speech of the mediator and apostle of the new testament is not for this present world or economy in any way. It is not to civilize it, change it, or better it: the gospel is to *deliver* from it, sanctifying those set free from the delusions of this world, preparing them inwardly and spiritually for that world which is to come.

The apostolic ministry of Christ cannot be adapted to this world. Where this is attempted, Paul calls it 'another gospel', a 'perversion of the gospel of Christ'. But in truth the new testament does not, and cannot, fit into this present world, nor can it possibly be suited to the worldly.

The entire moral structure of this world, the bent of its society, the bias of its fallen nature, the principles upon which it is operative, are all clean contrary both to the new testament, and to all that is effected by it. These things cannot be reconciled: they will not fit together, and they can never be made to fit together, world without end.

The apostolic ministry of the new testament; the heavenly voice of the Son of God from the glory; the presence and power of the Holy Ghost below and within; the doctrine of Christ in the gospel: all are to prepare the people of God for the holy city, sanctifying them inwardly to perfection, suiting them as the bride of Christ for the heavenly glory.

The new testament in itself and in those who receive it, is destined for another world, a new creation yet to come. It is designed for this, adapted to it. This is its purpose, and by its effectual indwelling in the saints, it transforms them within from fallen nature to the nature of Christ, and carries them out of this world into the next.

The gospel of Christ therefore pertains to a place beyond death; beyond the grave; beyond the dissolution; beyond the conflagration; beyond the resurrection; beyond the judgment:

finding its rest in the promised and everlasting inheritance of the saints.

This is the rest that remains for the people of God. As yet in vision, nevertheless the light of the glory illuminates and encourages the hearts of his own. Afar off they see a body of glory, of honour: incorruptible, immortal. They see the King in his beauty. They behold the light of the holy city, new Jerusalem; the kingdom to come; the new heavens and the new earth.

The new testament in the mouth of its apostle fits them for this coming glory. It is that for which his ministry is exercised. Receiving this gospel now, they are prepared for that glory then. They are being fashioned for the world to come even now upon the earth: being conformed to his image even at present throughout their sojourning in this alien world.

For this coming glory all their life is spent in hope whilst on earth. The cross is behind them; the glory is before them; and the Spirit is within them. This makes the distinction. It is the distinction of Christ and the gospel.

It is very evident that a new phase begins at Mark 9:30. 'They departed thence.' That was over. 'And passed through Galilee.' An entire phase of ministry had come to an end. He journeyed through, he did not tarry, he did not pass through to minister again. That was finished. Hence, 'He would not that any man should know it.'

That period had come to its conclusion. He travelled through, but privately. The past was not to be repeated. The public Galilean ministry was over. The beginning of the end was before him. And that end must needs be at Jerusalem.

Hence, immediately after recording 'He would not that any man should know it', the reason is given: 'For', Mk. 9:31. 'For': namely, the explanation of his actions follows.

'For he taught his disciples, and said unto them, The Son of man is delivered into the hands of men, and they shall kill him; and after that he is killed, he shall rise the third day.' The first of the things which he taught is repugnant to this world's society; and the last lies beyond its comprehension. But on both the kingdom is based.

Far from the ambitions which govern advancement in the society of this world, Jesus embodied and taught the opposite: 'For he *taught* his disciples' that which he exemplified. Far from using the unique anointing, authority, and power bestowed upon him to attain an earthly goal, or establish his kingdom in this life, it was the cross that was set before him. Crucifixion was his objective. The loss of his life was the purpose of his life.

Again, contrary to every motive in worldly society, and foreign to the life of the world, that which was set before Jesus was the life to come. The joy that is before the world is in this life; but the joy that was set before Jesus was after death. Therefore he endured the cross and despised the shame. But this was inconceivable to the world.

However Jesus lived for the glory. What lay beyond the resurrection was his motive and aim. Nothing in this life; nothing in this world; and nothing in this age: nothing but to die to it all. For him, everything was in the resurrection; everything was in the world to come; and everything was in eternity.

Moreover 'he taught them'. He taught his disciples the same principles, principles opposite to those which govern this world's society. And though his pathway—his vicarious pathway—was unique, it was none the less exemplary. 'My sheep hear my voice, and they follow me.' They follow in his steps. He is the forerunner, yes, but they are the following runners. His joy, their joy, was on the other side, the glory side, of death.

But, Mk. 9:32, 'They understood not that saying.' Nor would they, till he had died, risen again, ascended into glory, sent the Holy Ghost, and had begun the spiritual and interior administration of the new testament in their hearts and in their minds. For the time then present, 'They understood not that saying, and were afraid to ask him.'

Yet they understood the world's sayings, and were not afraid to ask each other. But he knew all things, and, when he came to Capernaum, being in the house, he enquired of them what he knew perfectly well: 'What was it that ye disputed among yourselves by the way?'

But they held their peace: for by the way they had disputed among themselves who should be the greatest. Whether or not they understood his saying, foretelling his shame, ignominy, and crucifixion—the opposite of the motive for their dispute— they understood enough of their own saying to feel so guilty that 'they held their peace'.

And he sat down, and called the twelve, and said unto them, If any man desire to be first, the same shall be last of all, and servant of all. Now this is the opposite of the driving motive of this world's society. But it is the distinction of Christ and the gospel. And it distinguishes those who aspire to a better resurrection.

And he took a child, and set him in the midst of them: and when he had taken him in his arms he said unto them, Whosoever shall receive one of such little children in my name, receiveth me: and whosoever shall receive me, receiveth not me, but him that sent me.

Seated in the midst of those who disputed who was the greatest, as they stood about him he cradled the little child in the arms of his affection. Neither able nor conscious of aspiration to the greatness sought by the awe-inspiring adults towering over him, the little child was not only the embodiment of the spirit that was in Jesus, but of the Father also. Now, here is the distinction of Christ and the gospel.

Reflecting upon the disciples' dispute, and Jesus' embracing the little child as their example, John is troubled as he recalls an incident in which the disciples rebuked one who had cast out demons in Jesus' name, forbidding him because 'he followeth not us'.

But what had been their motive? Evidently John felt it to be the desire to be the greatest. This gave rise to indignation against one not deferring to their prominence. John does not rise higher than the term 'Master', or teacher. Jesus, whilst not endorsing their action, nevertheless accepts and includes himself with their 'us'.

The reason the disciples ought not to forbid such persons is given: the miracle was done in Jesus' name. And if not following with 'us'—as he ought—nevertheless 'he that is not against us is on our part', Mk. 9:40. As to the disciples' deeper motive, the desire to be the greatest, this had been corrected by the incident of the little child.

As to those 'on our part', even if only giving a cup of water to the disciples, if it were—as was the casting out of demons—'in my name', none would lack reward. Why not? Because the disciples 'belong to Christ'.

If one cast out demons 'in my name'; if one give a cup of water to those who belong to Christ 'in my name': let the disciples beware. Though not yet of proper understanding, being but as little children, they are counted as 'little ones'—like the child cradled in Jesus' arms—and a woe is upon all who give offence to these.

Rather than give offence—or take offence—at Jesus' 'little ones', better to take offence against oneself. Better that a millstone were hanged about the neck of the offender, and he be cast into the sea.

If the offence given or taken concerned the work which one does, better to cut off the working member—the hand—and to enter into life maimed, than having two hands to go into hell, into the fire that never shall be quenched: where their worm dieth not, and the fire is not quenched.

If the offence given or taken concerned the pathway which one treads, better to cut off one's own foot, and enter halt into life, than having two feet to be cast into hell, into the fire that never shall be quenched: where their worm dieth not, and the fire is not quenched.

If the offence given or taken concerned the favour with which one is regarded, better to pluck out one's own eye and enter the kingdom of God with one eye, than having two eyes to be cast into hell fire: where their worm dieth not, and the fire is not quenched.

And where on earth—despite the impending punishment, threatened even to the disciples—where on earth, in any society of this world, will submission to such doctrine be found? It will be found nowhere, save among the 'little ones'. But these belong to a society other than this world.

Yet how shall such a nature be preserved in them, to whom by nature such humiliating self-denial is so contrary? By that which prevents the spread of corruption, and preserves the worth and savour of the new man. In a figure, Salt.

This used to be mingled with the sacrifices offered by fire under the old covenant. The salt burnt with the sacrifice. Salt itself provided a figure of what preserves from the corruption of the flesh, just as the fire signified what consumes the flesh. 'Little ones' submit to both—salt and fire—however painful and humiliating.

This pain, caused by the fire of providential afflictions, and the salt of inworking humiliations — fire and salt — was not applied for a moment; a day; a week; a month; or a year. It was for a lifetime. Not for the beginning of the pilgrimage; but for the whole of it. Otherwise the salt would have lost its savour.

Jesus arose from thence, and came into the coasts of Judea by the farther side of Jordan. There the people resorted to him—for he could not be hid—and there he taught them again.

The Pharisees come, not to hear his teaching, nor to enquire at his mouth, but to tempt him. Tempt him to do what? To contradict Moses, so that they could accuse him of antinomianism, that is, being against the law.

'Is it lawful for a man to put away his wife?' He knew their guile, and, going to the heart of it, pre-empted them by asking, 'What did Moses command you?' Answering question with question, Jesus' riposte anticipated their snare, had he given the answer they expected.

But he had found them out. For Moses *commanded* nothing. He *suffered* them to write a bill of divorcement, and to put her away. No more. And Jesus said, for the hardness of your heart he wrote you this precept. Hence, like all legalists they are discovered to be as full of guile as they were ignorant of Moses.

So hard were their hearts that, of old, they had cast out their wives without protection or provision. Nor were their wives any better when it pleased *them* to covet a new situation. The destitute and forsaken wife—or husband—originally had no recourse, being legally bound. But Moses, in compassion to the forsaken wife—or husband—suffered a bill of divorcement.

But it was not so from the beginning. It was a manifestation of subsequent depravity. Before the Fall, in the beginning, the man clave to his wife, and they twain were one flesh. What therefore God hath joined together, let not man put asunder. And what could the Pharisees reply to that?

In the house—which house, in Judea beyond Jordan, if this be not an allusion to the Son over his own house, the house of God? — the disciples sought elucidation of this matter, Mk. 10:10.

They received it unequivocally. Whoso shall put away his wife, and marry another, committeth adultery against her. And if a woman shall put away her husband, and be married to another, she committeth adultery. Legal provision for a hard-hearted world therefore had no place in the house of God amongst little children.

In the next passage, Mk. 10:13-16, three times the little children are mentioned. They brought young children to Jesus that he should touch them. The disciples, still governed by the principles of this world in the matter, pompously rebuked those who did so: the great teacher should not be troubled by such trifling. But the heart of it was their own self-importance.

When Jesus saw it he was much displeased, and said unto them, Suffer the little children to come unto me. Would they never learn that the self-importance, the disputing for greatness, the ambition for status, lying at the heart of this world's society, was in clean contrast to that which obtained in the kingdom of God?

Verily, saith he, Whosoever shall not receive the kingdom of God as a little child—a little child being so void of that which had been exhibited by the disciples on this occasion also—he shall not enter therein. And he took them up in his arms, and put his hands upon them, and blessed them.

Next follows the incident of one who came running, kneeling to Jesus, asking him, Good Master, what shall I do that I may inherit eternal life? Answering the man according to his perceptions, Jesus refers goodness to God alone. Then what could *man* do to be good enough, as he supposed, to earn or merit eternal life?

Since the man sought life by works, Jesus enumerates the commandments. Alive without the law, the young man was convinced he had done all that was required from his youth up. Then why had he no life? But Jesus deliberately omitted one commandment from the second table which he had quoted. It was this: Thou shalt not covet.

However the man did covet, for he could not bear to be parted from his great possessions. Jesus, leaving the law, putting all on a gospel footing, informs him that he should sell all, give to the poor, and come, take up the cross, and follow him. But this he could not bring himself to do.

And Jesus looked round about—then, on his disciples—and said, How hardly shall they that have riches enter into the kingdom of God. His disciples were astonished. Jesus said to them, Children, how hard is it for them that trust in riches to enter into the kingdom of God.

Such neither keep the law—for trusting in riches, they covet them, but, Thou shalt not covet—nor do they embrace Christ and the gospel—for, trusting in riches, they dare not leave all and follow him. Why not? Because they embody the spirit of this world's society, and there is a distinction.

Peter began to say unto Jesus, Lo, we have left all, and have followed thee. And, for all their lapses—for the Holy Ghost was not yet given—this was transparently true. And Jesus comforts them, assuring them not only regarding eternal life, but, after they had suffered a while, even this present life, Mk. 10:28-31.

And they were in the way going up to Jerusalem; and Jesus went before them: and they were amazed; and as they followed, they were afraid. And he took again the twelve, and began to tell them what things should happen unto him.

And he said, Behold, we go up to Jerusalem; and the Son of man shall be delivered unto the chief priests, and unto the scribes; and they shall condemn him to death, and shall deliver him to the Gentiles: and they shall mock him, and shall scourge him, and shall spit upon him, and shall kill him: and the third day he shall rise again.

Amazed and troubled, the disciples felt that the way Jesus took was bound to end in ignominy, shame, and death. Yet here he confirms it. This would be the end of all their hopes. The end of everything in Israel, and the end of their expectation in the present world. To them, his anointing, his power, his unique authority from God, were being deliberately cast away.

There was a distinction between Christ and the gospel, and this world's society, that, even now—despite the way that he took—they could not comprehend.

Hence James and John come to him—after all that he had taught them but a moment ago—and sought to sit on Jesus' right and left hand in his glory. What is this but circumventing the dispute among themselves, by a direct approach to Jesus, that they might be counted the greatest?

Jesus tells them that they knew not what they asked. Can they drink of his cup? Can they partake of his baptism? In their folly they affirm that they can. But he agrees. Only, he should drink the cup of wrath alone, and be baptized beneath the waters of death vicariously. Then they should drink his cup of blessing; and then they should find themselves baptized together with Christ in his death.

163

Not otherwise. The ten, who had shared with them the earlier dispute as to who should be the greatest, were much displeased at this going to Jesus behind their backs. But Jesus showed them, this should not advantage James and John, any more than their dispute would promote one above another. The very principle, common to the world, was contrary to the kingdom.

They which are accounted to rule over the Gentiles exercise lordship over them; and their great ones exercise authority upon them. But so shall it not be among you: but whosoever will be great among you, shall be your minister: and whosoever of you will be the chiefest, shall be servant of all. Here is distinction with a witness.

And they came to Jericho, and as he went out of Jericho with his disciples and a great number of people, blind Bartimaeus, the son of Timaeus, sat by the highway side begging. He cried aloud, 'Jesus, thou son of David, have mercy on me'.

Supposing—according to the principles of this world's ranking — Jesus to be too important a person, what with all his disciples, and so great a multitude, many told the blind beggar to shut up. But they were wrong. Their standard of judgment was wrong: for he considered the poor. And he stood still, and commanded him to be brought.

And he—who had named Jesus the Son of David—casting away his garment, rose, and came unto him. And Jesus answered and said unto him, What wilt thou that I should do unto thee? The blind man said unto him, Lord, that I might receive my sight. Son of David? Lord? This faith is the consequence of both a prior work, and of the revelation of the Father from heaven.

And Jesus said unto him, Go thy way; thy faith hath made thee whole. Go thy way? But he followed Jesus in the way. Well, what else had he in the world? By which it is evident that there is a distinction. The society of this world is one thing. But pilgrims and strangers, with nothing in this world, are another thing. That is the distinction of Christ and the gospel.

ii. It is not for this world's religion

This world's religion stood under the old covenant; God's choice of Israel; the works of the law; a worldly sanctuary; an earthly inheritance; a blessing on obedience and a curse on disobedience: all of which obtained for this life only.

After centuries these original institutes had become submerged beneath traditions; usurped by hypocrites; corrupted by the scribes; and perverted by the successive generations of those who had received that which had been handed down to them from their fathers.

The centre of this religion was at Jerusalem; its coasts were the boundaries of Israel; and its ideal was the proselytizing of this world to the ends of the earth.

At last—and for the first and only time in Mark—Jesus came up to Jerusalem, to the house of God therein, to the sanctuary, to bear witness to the truth. This climactic witness appears in chapters 11 and 12.

Just as—according to the law—in the mouth of two or three witnesses every matter should be established, so the witness of the mediator and apostle of the new testament appears over three consecutive days. This is not recorded by Matthew and Luke, each of whom records two days only. The witness over three days is exclusive to Mark.

The chief priests, the scribes, and the elders—indeed the entire Sanhedrin—ought joyfully to have welcomed the coming of Christ and the gospel to a system of religion that was never intended to be other than interim, and which, during the long centuries of interval, had failed palpably. But they did not. They hated his coming. They rejected the new testament. And they detested his witness. But he gave it none the less.

The account of the first day—and, therefore, of Jesus' first entry into Jerusalem and the temple—appears in chapter 11, verses 1 to 11.

'And when they came nigh to Jerusalem, unto Bethphage and Bethany, at the mount of Olives, he sendeth forth two of his disciples, and saith unto them, Go your way into the village over against you: and as soon as ye be entered into it, ye shall find a colt tied, whereon never man sat; loose him, and bring him', Mk. 11:1,2.

They did so, finding the colt tied by the door without in a place where two ways met; and they loose him. As Jesus had forewarned, those standing by questioned what they were doing. As Jesus had commanded them, so they replied. And they let them go.

This reveals a remarkable divine providence on the one hand, and an extraordinary prophetic foreknowledge on the other. One should observe not only how much had been divinely ordained; nor simply that Jesus knew exactly what would take place, down to the words that were to be spoken; but that he knew all this well before the event. Consider also the situation, pregnant with meaning.

A place where two ways met. The whole atmosphere, the climax of centuries, the very air vibrant with divine purpose: here two ways met with a witness. The old covenant met with the new; the law met with the gospel; the shadow met with the substance; earth met with heaven; time met with eternity; and the servants met with the Son.

But meeting, these things crossed. The meeting did not linger: two *ways* met, and, meeting, passed on. One to eternal judgment and everlasting perdition. The other to free justification and glorious immortality.

And they brought the colt to Jesus, and cast their garments on him; and he sat upon him. And many spread their garments in the way, and strawed branches in the way. And they that went before, and they that followed, cried, saying, Hosanna; Blessed is he that cometh in the name of the Lord: Blessed be the kingdom of our father David, that cometh in the name of the Lord: Hosanna in the highest.

And Jesus entered into Jerusalem, and into the temple: and when he had looked round about upon all things, and now the eventide was come, he went out unto Bethany with the twelve.

Jesus did nothing. But in the temple there was nothing that he did not observe. Not a word passed his lips throughout that day. But not a detail escaped his observation from dawn till dusk. This was the first day of his witness. It is unique to Mark.

On this day the messenger of the covenant — the new covenant—suddenly came to his temple. John had been sent before him, to prepare his way. Every sign had been given; every prophecy, all scripture, fulfilled; now at last he had come up to Jerusalem, suddenly to his temple.

But if he said not a word, neither did they. If the crowds had heralded his coming, the chief priests, scribes, and elders had not. Not a word. 'And when he had'—all that day—'looked round about upon all things, and now the eventide was come, he went out.'

The significance of that day, etched in time: the passing of its hours into history; the dropping of its moments into eternity;

at last the failing of its light; the ticking away of its final seconds: these things can never be forgotten. They are written in the book of God for ever. But the day was lost on the rulers of the Jews. Came the darkness, and their day was past.

The events of the second day—and, therefore, of Jesus' second entry into Jerusalem and the temple—stand recorded in chapter 11, verses 12 to 19.

On the journey from Bethany early in the morning, hungry, Jesus saw a fig tree afar off having leaves. It seemed at a distance as if it would bear fruit. But when Jesus came to it, just as yesterday he had come to the temple, he found no fruit. There was nothing but leaves.

'And Jesus answered and said unto it', Mk. 11:14. Jesus answered? As if its outward show of leaves—but actual barrenness—had *spoken*? But it had spoken: just as the things seen yesterday had spoken. And this was Jesus' answer to both: Jesus said unto *it*. But why, if it were not symbolic of the momentous events that had taken place, and would take place?

'No man eat fruit of thee hereafter for ever', Mk. 11:14. Here is a perpetual curse. It is irrevocable. There was nothing impetuous about it: 'He came, if haply he might find anything thereon: and when he came to it, he found nothing but leaves.' He came; he saw; he judged. Just as he had done yesterday. He found no fruit. Just as he found no fruit yesterday. But barrenness in the day of reckoning brought down judgment in perpetuity.

This was *before* Jesus' second entry into Jerusalem. All was settled. On this, the second day, Jesus went directly into the temple and began immediately to cast out them that bought and sold in the temple, overthrowing the tables of the money-changers, and the seats of them that sold doves.

And he would not suffer that any man should carry any vessel through the temple. All kinds of money passed hands between every sort of buyer and seller. Jews from far countries changed their foreign currency at the convenient money-changers. Distant travellers from the diaspora, unable to bring sacrifices, found a trade ready to hand for the purpose.

And whoever would, used the precincts as a shortcut, carrying their vessels from one entrance to another exit.

The chief priests, the scribes, and the elders looked on at this traffic benignly. It was all profit, and religion and its fabric needed every financial assistance to shore up its structures against the march of time. Not only did the hierarchy turn a blind eye to everything, the entire extraneous growth of trade was tacitly encouraged.

But Jesus threw it all down, cast it all out, and forbad the entire blasphemous procedure, saying 'Is it not written, My house shall be called of all nations the house of *prayer*? but ye have made it a den of thieves', Mk. 11:17.

And the scribes and chief priests heard it, and sought how they might destroy him: for they feared him, because all the people was astonished at his doctrine.

And when the even was come, he went out of the city.

The record of the final day—and, therefore of Jesus' third entry into Jerusalem and the temple—follows in chapter 11:20 through to the end of chapter 12.

In the morning, as they passed by, they saw the fig tree dried up from the roots. And so the previous two days had proved to be the case with Israel and the Jews. This world's religion was not only barren and fruitless, it was dried up from the roots. It was impossible for sap ever to rise again through that dead wood.

But from those ancient roots, God had chosen Israel, enjoined unto them the old covenant, having delivered the law by the disposition of angels. But now Israel proved to be a veritable mountain in the way of the bringing in of the new testament.

Said Jesus, Verily I say unto you, That whosoever shall say unto this mountain, Be thou removed, and be thou cast into the sea; and shall not doubt in his heart, but shall believe that those things which he saith shall come to pass; he shall have whatsoever he saith.

And so he proved in himself. The corrupt custodians of the temple; the perverse traditions of the elders; and the hypocrisy of the Jews—with their entire worldly religion—were dried up from the roots at Jesus' word.

Moreover in justice he took away the mountain of God's having given the first covenant, lawfully delivering from that mount Sinai of God's appointing, whilst righteously breaking off the natural branches of Israel, yet honouring the true stock of God's eternal election.

Having taught his disciples in the way, they came again to Jerusalem, and Jesus walked in the temple. On this day, first he was to encounter and silence three representatives of this world's religion; then two such representatives; next one entire sect; and finally an individual who had come as far as seemed possible under the old covenant.

Seven parties: four occasions. Perfect representation of all that the flesh and the natural man can do in this world's religion, both before, during, and after the event, to the world's end. Each one in turn is convicted and silenced by the Spirit and by the word of the apostle of the heavenly, spiritual, glorious and everlasting new testament.

First there came to him the chief priests, and the scribes, and the elders, Mk. 11:27. They—who considered authority to be vested in their offices, and therefore themselves—accost Jesus and challenge his right to do what he had done on the second day of entry: 'By what authority doest thou these things? and who gave thee this authority?'

They had not. Therefore, resting on the dignity and weight of their station, they challenge Jesus' neglect of their permission, and, as they supposed, the absence of any authorization for his actions. For to the hierarchy, God had no voice other than theirs, and handed down no command other than by them.

First the chief priests: these were the heads of a sacramental system of continual and repetitive sacrifice. They were ordained in Aaron. However, this world's religion still retains this system, long after its temporary significance has passed away with the old testament. For repetitive sacrifices declare in their very nature that sin had not been taken away.

The scribes were supposed to be the custodians of scripture. But the reality of their custody lay in the traditions with which they had overlaid the scripture. They had made void the word of God by their traditions.

Finally in this group were the elders. They were the previous generation, now old men, holding on for all their worth. Being old, it was all reminiscence and repetition. Demanding subjection on account of their age and office, they force their traditions on the young: 'Why transgress ye the tradition of the elders?'

These weighed their authority against Jesus, the Son of God, the mediator and apostle of the new testament. And, for all their status, their dignity, and their venerable appearance, Jesus' words leave them exposed and speechless, for 'he taught as one *having* authority, and not as the scribes'.

'The baptism of John', he asks, 'was it from heaven, or of men? answer.' They are caught. All the people counted John for a

171

prophet indeed. But he had testified of Jesus. If they denied that, the crowds round about would laugh them to scorn. If they agreed to it, Jesus would say, Why then did ye not believe him?

And they answered and said, We cannot tell. And Jesus answered, Neither do I tell you by what authority I do these things, Mk. 11:33.

And he began to speak unto them by parables. Specifically, the parable of the vineyard, Mk. 12:1-12. A certain man planted a vineyard, hedged it, prepared it, built about it, and let it out to husbandmen. Then he departed.

Annually seeking fruits, year after year his messengers were rejected, stoned, wounded, shamefully handled, and even slain. However, having one son, last of all he sent him also. They said, 'This is the heir; come, let us kill him, and the inheritance shall be ours.'

The chief priests, and the scribes, and the elders, knew what he meant: 'They knew that he had spoken the parable against them', Mk. 12:12. And was it a question of authority? Then who gave them this authority, and by what authority did they these things? They were but servants. He was the Son. And his was the inheritance.

But they would do even as it was written of them, and as Jesus foretold. They would kill him. At that very time 'they sought to lay hold on him, but feared the people', Mk. 12:12. However their murderous act would profit them nothing. The Lord of that vineyard will 'destroy the husbandmen, and will give the vineyard unto others', Mk. 12:9.

He will give the vineyard unto others in a mystery, as it is written in the scripture quoted by Jesus, 'The stone which the builders rejected is become the head of the corner'. It is he himself, risen from the dead, who has become chief corner stone in the house of God not made with hands, that is, the *ecclesia* of the living God.

Frustrated, they go. But they send others. 'And they send unto him certain of the Pharisees and of the Herodians, to catch him in his words', Mk. 12:13. The Pharisees were avowed separatists. But not upon divine principles, which admittedly teach separation. But the ground of separation for the Pharisee was this: 'Stand thou by me, for I am holier than thou.'

Then whatever were these doing with the Herodians? What? with 'a political Jewish party that favoured Greek customs'? Yet God had judged their fathers for this very same reason: 'They were mingled among the heathen, and learned their works. And they served their idols: which were a snare unto them.'

These were the sworn enemies of the Pharisees, yet both found common cause against Jesus, who by his heavenly conversation and spiritual words showed up every manifestation that the flesh could assume under a religious guise. Hence those who were of the flesh found an affinity in their mutual enmity against Jesus, uniting together under the chief priests, scribes, and elders, 'to catch him in his words'.

First they flatter him: 'Master, we know that thou art true, and carest for no man: for thou regardest not the person of men, but teachest the way of God in truth.' But 'with flattering lips and with a double heart do they speak', Ps. 12:2. It is only that they might 'catch him in his words' that they use flattery, vainly supposing to put him off guard.

Next they think to draw him on: 'Is it lawful to give tribute to Caesar, or not?' Here is the worldly sophistication of the Herodians mixed with the crafty guile of the Pharisees. 'They search out iniquities; they accomplish a diligent search: both the inward thought of every one of them, and the heart, is deep', Ps. 64:6.

If he should say, Give to Caesar; they would reply that this is to yield unlawfully to the heathen that have come into God's inheritance. If he should say, Give not to Caesar; they would report him for teaching rebellion against the Roman authority. One was a religious transgression, the other a civil offence. But, holding the penny he had been given, he asked, Whose image and superscription is this?

Puzzled, they reply, Caesar's. And Jesus answering said unto them, Render to Caesar the things that are Caesar's, and to God the things that are God's. So *that* was why he had asked them for the penny. Then who is caught in whose words? And they marvelled at him, Mk. 12:17.

Next there came to him the Sadducees, the third group, and the sixth party, whose traits, together with—but distinct from— each of the seven, will always appear under some guise or another in contemporary religion. These are the fathers of liberal theology. No angels, no Spirit, no resurrection, no inspiration. Rational modernists, these gently disbelieve, with a kindly and loving tolerance.

This party denies everything that does not originate with man: no miracles, no divinity, no creation, no flood, and, in modern terms, no Moses and no scripture. In place of Moses they have J., E., P., and D. Instead of the sure text of scripture they have the unstable theorizing of Westcott and Hort.

In the contemporary manifestation of this party, they have no virgin birth, no eternal Sonship, no one God in three Persons, and no three Persons in one God. No immortality, no bodily resurrection, no judgment, no world to come. The marvel about these people is, Why bother? Answer, Because there is a place to their advantage in the wide spectrum of the religion of this world.

Coming to Jesus, the Sadducees lightly and frivolously jest about the resurrection with dubious taste and blind ignorance,

Mk. 12:18-23. Of the seven successive brethren who had the woman to wife—as Moses commanded—on the death of his brother, Which should have her in the resurrection?

But they did not believe in the resurrection. Nor did they credit Moses. So why snigger such things to Jesus? Because at heart they were as opposed and full of enmity against his heavenly spirituality and divine anointing as any other of the seven parties representing all the forms of this world's religion.

But Jesus rebuked them: 'Ye do *greatly* err.' And what was their error? 'Because ye know not the scriptures, neither the power of God.' And that is at the root of the malaise of every Sadducee—called by whatever contemporary name—that ever existed.

The power of God in the resurrection is not exerted to bring in this world once more, or man after the flesh again. It is to bring in the world to come, and man in Christ, at once spiritual, glorious, heavenly, and mysterious: as the angels that are in heaven. And what divine power does that require? and what do they know of this mystery?

The scriptures—which they knew not—recorded by Moses—whom they believed not—tell of God speaking unto Moses in the bush, saying, I am the God of Abraham, and the God of Isaac, and the God of Jacob. Not, I *was* the God of Abraham, Isaac, and Jacob: I *am.*

Yet when God spake these words to Moses, the patriarchs Abraham, Isaac, and Jacob had been dead—as to the body—these hundreds of years. Nevertheless—as to the soul—the living God refers to them as immortal: I *am* the God of Abraham, Isaac, and Jacob. If so, at that same time.

Then, the soul being incomplete without the body, their living souls bear mute testimony to a coming resurrection of their slumbering remains. For, 'He is not the God of the dead, but the God of the living: ye therefore do greatly err', Mk. 12:27.

Finally one of the scribes — a party which had already appeared together with the chief priests and the elders—brings to a close the sevenfold and perfect manifestation of all that religion can possibly effect in any circumstances, generation, or age. For there are those of the scribes who appear to be more noble—in consequence of the religion of this world—than their contemporaries.

One of these, having heard Jesus' answer to the Sadducees, asked, Which is the first commandment of all? Mk. 12:28. The man came to the heart of the law, and from the heart of the gospel he is answered. For the truth is, none of those under the law knows the law: neither by doctrine nor in experience. But those in Christ and under grace know the law: both by doctrine and in experience.

Jesus informs the scribe that to love the Lord thy God with all thy heart, soul, mind, and strength is the first commandment. The second is like unto it, namely, thou shalt love thy neighbour as thyself. There is none other commandment greater than these, Mk. 12:30,31.

The scribe moderately agrees, as if to confirm this answer given to him by the Son who made the worlds, gave the law by the disposition of angels, came into the world as the mediator and apostle of the new testament, who *was* the truth, and who is called, Christ, the wisdom of God, of whom John says, He was with God, and was God.

But the meekness of Christ absorbs the impudence of man, and he tells the scribe, 'Thou art not far from the kingdom of God', Mk. 12:34. No, not far: as far as the law and works, the religion of this world, could bring him. Not so far as the vail: only the high priest could come that far. Not so far as the entrance: only the priests came to the entrance.

He came as far as the court. But it was not because of that; or his law; or his own works; that he was not far from the kingdom. For the law hid Jehovah; it vailed the LORD; it set God infinitely beyond impenetrable darkness. Not far?

He was not far from the kingdom because, in that courtyard of the temple, he was speaking to the King, who held the kingdom in himself. That far. But he knew nothing of that, this scribe blinded by the law.

'But even unto this day, when Moses is read, the vail is upon their heart', II Cor. 3:15. The obscurity of that thick vail altogether prevented his seeing the King and the kingdom from which he was—then—not far. But far enough: for all his law, and his condescending agreement, he knew neither the law, nor the gospel. No more had he the least inclination to reach out his hand and touch the kingdom of God.

'But if our gospel be hid'—and it *was* hid from the scribe—'it is hid to them that are lost: in whom the god of this world hath blinded the minds of them which believe not, lest the light of the glorious gospel of Christ, who is the image of God, should shine unto them', II Cor. 4:3,4.

Wherefore it is evident that at its very best, there is neither light, life, love, divinity, nor worship in all the religion that is of this world, no, not in any one of its manifestations, though all should be sought out to perfection.

And no man after that durst ask him any question, Mk. 12:34. But Jesus asked them one question: 'How say the scribes that Christ is the Son of David? For David himself said by the Holy Ghost, The LORD'—that is in capitals: it is JEHOVAH—'said to my Lord'—this is not in capitals: it is *Adonai*—'Sit thou on my right hand, till I make thine enemies thy footstool.'

Now, here is a distinction of divine Persons in the indivisible unity of the deity. And what will the scribes, blinded under the law, make of that?

Or of this: 'David therefore himself calleth him'—whom? Why, his son, Christ, the son of David; that is the question: How say the scribes that Christ is the *son* of David?—David 'calleth him Lord; and whence is he then his son?' No father calls his son *Adonai*, or Lord and Master. It is for a son to do that to a father. But David did it to Christ, his *Adonai*.

'How then is he his son?' The answer is that there are three Persons in one God, and one God in three Persons; Father, Son, and Holy Ghost, from eternity to eternity. But it pleased God to send his Son. He was made of the seed of David according to the flesh. Now David in spirit *knew* who his son should be, calling him, Lord. Why not the scribes?

'And the common people heard him gladly', Mk. 12:37. And Jesus said unto them in his doctrine, 'Beware of the scribes'— why in particular? Because, of all the manifestations of the flesh in this world's religion, those of the more moral, scriptural appearance are the most deceptive—'Beware of the scribes.' That is the first thing.

The next follows: they love to go in long clothing: or at least, an appearance distinctive enough to mark them out; they love salutations in the market-places: or at least, deference distinctive enough to ensure that they are noticed.

The scribes love the chief seats in the synagogue: or at least, flattery distinctive enough in the assembly to be honoured of man; they love the uppermost rooms at feasts: or at least, elevation distinctive enough to be had in praise for their religious importance. And with all this fourfold love of the world, what room can be left for the scribes to 'love the Lord thy God with *all* thy heart', Mk. 12:30?

No room can exist in the heart of these, for they love the praise of man more than the praise of God. They are hypocrites. They were hypocrites then, and they are hypocrites now. But deceptive hypocrites, for their worldliness is hidden behind their coat of whitewash. But their covetousness cannot be hid: 'Which devour widows' houses, and for a pretence make long prayers', Mk. 12:40.

'These shall receive greater damnation.' Greater than that of whom? Greater than that of the gullible and deceived people who congregate to follow these blind leaders of the blind. Both receive damnation, but the scribes' is greater.

Just how much men are deceived by appearances in this world's religion abundantly manifests itself as Jesus sat over against the treasury. Here he watched the almsgivers casting in their offerings with sanctified air and gesture. He discerned all: and the measure of his judgment lay in his distinguishing between what was done to be seen of man, and what was not.

An unremarkable poor widow threw in two mites. Who looked? Jesus looked. 'And he called unto him his disciples, and saith unto them, Verily I say unto you, That this poor widow hath cast more in, than all they which have cast into the treasury.' In his eyes, there was a distinction.

'For all they did cast in of their abundance; but she of her want did cast in all that she had, even all her living', Mk. 12:44. Her two mites were more valued by the Son of God, than the entire sum of every abundant gift.

For that which is highly esteemed among men is abomination in the sight of God. And that which is of no weight in the sight of men is highly esteemed in the balances of the sanctuary. Here is the distinction: that which pertains to the sight of man belongs to this world's religion. And that which pertains to the sight of God belongs to Christ and the gospel.

iii. *It is not for this world's duration*

Having silenced every shade of religious opinion, and prophesied against every sect, division, and party of man's devising in this world's religion, foretelling its destruction—of which Judaism was shortly to be an example—Jesus leaves the temple.

His threefold testimony had been delivered. Judaism had been weighed in the balances, and found wanting. This world's religion and its religious had been exposed, and its false worship rejected by the mediator and apostle of the new testament.

One thing remained. Leaving the temple, the occasion was provided by the foolish remark of a disciple, awe-struck by the grandeur of the temple buildings. Jesus thereupon foretells the destruction of the temple, and the sinking of all hope of Jewry as a nation and people in the counsels of God.

From which it follows of course that the entire fabric of premillennialism is annihilated, since not a shred of evidence for it exists here or elsewhere. How could it? This passage, as it must, teaches the very opposite, destroying from the root that pestilential error which overturns every principle of grace.

In a sense the awe-struck disciple displayed the seeds of premillennialism. He appears to have understood nothing whatsoever of the significance of the three-day testimony. All that he could do was gawp and exclaim at the supposed permanence of the Jewish system, set forth in the temple buildings, Mk. 13:1.

'Jesus answering said unto him, Seest thou these great buildings? there shall not be left one stone upon another, that shall not be thrown down', Mk. 13:2. By this rebuke, Jesus destroys the very seeds of error clutched by the ignorant, agog with admiration, gazing at earthly things, whether the temple, the people, or the inheritance.

The old covenant had run its course; Judaism had been judged; their house had been left unto them desolate. 'No man eat fruit of thee hereafter for ever.' Nevertheless the glorious gospel, administered from heaven by the ascended Son, must go—in the individual sense—'to the Jew first', that the spiritual seed of Abraham might find true peace in the gospel of Christ.

Later that day, privately Jesus answered the questions of four brethren as they sat upon the mount of Olives, over against the temple. 'When shall these things be? and what shall be the sign when all these things shall be fulfilled?' His reply soared over, above, and beyond the questions, although in the process he gave adequate response to their immediate enquiry.

But it is not just the temple: it was this world's religion. It is not just Judaism: it was man in the flesh concerning the things of God. It is not just a period of time: it was time itself. It was the duration of this world's religion. From their limited preoccupation, Jesus' transcendent vision ascends to scan time itself till the last day. It soars to enlarge upon the principles of his testimony delivered in the midst of this world's religion.

His testimony? But this testimony would continue from heaven. He would speak through his apostles on earth. He would extend that witness by his sending subsequent ministers of the apostles' doctrine till the end of the age. Thus he answered. And only thus can his answer be understood.

His answer is directed to principles. It traces those principles as first applied to the events leading up to and including the destruction of Jerusalem. But then, running on to the end of the age, the same principles are applied to the religion of this world—now Christendom—from the overturning of the temple even until the coming again of Christ.

In all this there appears the heavenly continuation of his own apostolic witness. First by his faithful apostles, both before,

181

during, and after the destruction of the temple and of Jerusalem, and then in the following apostolic ministry, testified before the rulers and kings of the Gentiles, the gospel being preached to all nations.

The exposure of the inherent rottenness of worldly religion—by no means limited to the temple and its system during Jesus' three days testimony—would follow hard upon the heels of the spread of the gospel to the Gentiles. Swiftly the growth of the apostasy should increase, overcoming all Christendom, just as Israel had been overwhelmed by the same corruption.

However, as God did to the Jews in their day, so he would do to Christendom in its day. He sends messengers, again, and again, and again. With what result? 'The brother shall betray the brother, the father the son; and children shall rise up against their parents, and shall cause them to be put to death.'

'And ye shall be hated of all men for my name's sake', Mk. 13:13. That is, the faithful ministers of Christ would testify of the mediatorial and apostolic speech of the Son from the glory, likewise bearing witness of his denunciation against the religion of this world and its worldly ministers, throughout the duration of the age. *These* are the witnesses which shall be hated of all men for his name's sake.

The course of this age should be marked increasingly by man's corruption of Christ's testimony rendered in the beginning, and of the apostolic word delivered after his ascension. Of that corruption the faithful are neither to be ignorant nor silent. They are not to suffer those who under the name of tolerance pretend that this apostasy is other than it is, namely, the same as that of the Jews rebuked by Jesus at the first.

Although the exterior unfoldings and earthly circumstances of the age should become increasingly alarming, the faithful are to hold steady, remaining unmoved—having been fore-warned—by the corruption of the testimony, the deterioration of what was from the beginning, the falling away of many, and the false claims arising from this world's religion. See Mk. 13:5-8.

These things are the beginning of sorrows. In the light of this, and of what is to come, Jesus admonishes his apostolic ministers to endure all things faithfully to the end, Mk. 13:9-13. As the testimony increases to all nations, Christ's witnesses shall be delivered up to councils, beaten in synagogues or assemblies, and brought before rulers or kings for a testimony against them.

The testimony of Christ's faithful and apostolic ministry neither accommodates this world nor its religion. It answers entirely to the voice of the Son of God from heaven, speaking by the Holy Ghost in his faithful servants below: 'for it is not ye that speak, but the Holy Ghost', Mk. 13:11. This speech in principle answers precisely to that of Jesus during his three days of witness in the temple at Jerusalem on earth.

Delivered to councils; beaten in the assemblies; taken before rulers and kings for a testimony against them; led away; delivered up; hated; slain: 'but he that shall endure unto the end, the same shall be saved.' This is the course of Christ's testimony, particularly in the apostolic ministry, but generally among all the saints.

Returning to the question of the four brethren, rather than the apostolic testimony throughout the age, Jesus refers to the impending destruction of Jerusalem, Mk. 13:14-23.

However, even this is put in such a way that the words of prophecy extend to the persecution of all the elect, till the end of days. Through everything the elect are to hold fast and endure, even unto death. It was certain that unprecedented suffering should precede the rising up of false apostles, deceitful ministers, and false Christs, from the religion of this world.

'But take ye heed: behold, I have foretold you all things.' *All* things. Not just the destruction of the temple; the sacking of Jerusalem; the condemnation of Judaism: but drawing from these things, the entire course of the testimony, throughout time, even to the end of the age. For principles must hold good, whatever the period. Save only, the recurring cycles of tribulation should increase more and more upon each return.

The corruption of Christendom would be apparent from the beginning; but it should ferment like leaven, until the whole was leavened. False representations of Christ and his doctrine would appear even then; but these will be nothing compared to their proliferation as the consummation of all things drew nigh.

The temple would fall amidst dreadful afflictions. However this should pale into insignificance compared to that attending the fall of Christendom in the coming days of unprecedented tribulation.

Nevertheless the elect are forewarned of the certainty that despite these signs the end is not yet. Not whilst the earth trembles. But when the heavens change, then the end is nigh. During the former times tribulation will trouble the whole world, to mount increasingly as the new—heavenly—portents loom nearer and nearer, Mk. 13:24-27.

Intensifying tribulation on earth; furious persecutions in the world and from its hostile religion; dreadful global visitations. But the end is not yet. The elect must endure all with patience, expecting no relief, knowing that this is but the herald of new signs in a different and heavenly sphere.

'The sun shall be darkened, and the moon shall not give her light. And the stars of heaven shall fall, and the powers that are in heaven shall be shaken.' Then; mark that, *then*— not till then—'Then shall they see the Son of man coming in the clouds with great power and glory', Mk. 13:26.

There is no secret, hidden, rapture here: nor anywhere else. The grievous error of premillennialism is shown up once again for the fabrication that it is. Here is the second coming of Christ, prophesied whilst on the mount of Olives during his first coming. These are the portents of his coming again, and it is the only coming again.

When the earthly portents reach their peak in time, then the heavenly portents herald the imminence of the second coming of Christ. 'Then'—after the heavenly portents have shaken all that is above—Then shall 'they' see the Son of man coming in the clouds with great power and glory.

But who is 'they'? Evidently not the four brethren to whom Jesus uttered this prophecy. Neither their faithful brethren even to this last hour. For such would be—as it appears throughout the prophecy—referred to as 'you'. That is, his own.

But it is not 'you'. It is 'they'. Namely, the world, and the world's religion. *They* shall see him coming in the clouds with great power and glory. All the world, and the entirety of the worldly religious. They hated Christ's elect. They persecuted them. But he loved his elect. He cherished them. And now he has come to vindicate and avenge them.

'And then'—when the world, and its religion, have seen his coming in the clouds with great power and glory—'then shall he send his angels, and shall gather together his elect from the four winds, from the uttermost part of the earth to the uttermost part of heaven', Mk. 13:27. And so shall they ever be with the Lord.

The elect being raised from the dead, delivered out of the world, gathered to Christ in his glory, nothing remains for the world, and for this world's religion, but the fiery deluge, the dissolution of all things, the resurrection of damnation, the final judgment, and the vengeance of eternal fire.

Then what have the saints to fear in all the afflictions, tribulations, and persecutions that attend this short and passing pilgrimage? 'Our light affliction, which is but for a moment, *worketh for us* a far more exceeding and eternal weight of glory', II Cor. 4:17. Our light affliction works for us: it keeps us low; it keeps us mortified; and it keeps us from temptation.

In experience therefore the elect have long bidden adieu to the world: its pleasures; its seductions; its society; and its religion, in every manifestation of its entire system. Crucifixion—'The world is crucified unto me, and I unto the world', Gal. 6:14—the daily cross, self-denial, following Christ, abiding in him: this is what marks out the pilgrims and strangers.

The elect have long settled the matter in their hearts, that, like the Son of man, death is not only their destiny but their goal in this world and its religion. Death to it; death from it; and death out of it. 'While we look not at the things which are seen, but at the things which are not seen: for the things which are seen are temporal; but the things which are not seen are eternal', II Cor. 4:18.

The saints look beyond the death which is all that they expect and anticipate in and from this world. They look for a better resurrection the other side of death; they look for the glory the other side of the grave; they look for an inheritance in the world to come, when this world—and all its religion—sinks into everlasting perdition.

Since this is the destiny of the elect, and because tribulation is their sole earthly expectation, they endure to the end, notwithstanding all the sufferings and persecution which they encounter throughout the days of their pilgrimage. Neither the signs on earth, nor yet the portents in the heaven make them to fear. Rather they rejoice that these things signify their hearts' joy: Christ is soon, so soon, coming back for them.

'Now learn a parable of the fig tree; When her branch is yet tender, and putteth forth leaves, ye know that summer is near:

186

so ye in like manner, when ye shall see these things come to pass, know that it is nigh, even at the doors', Mk. 13:28,29.

'Take ye heed, watch and pray: for ye know not when the time is. For the Son of man is as a man taking a far journey, who left his house, and gave authority to his servants, and to every man his work, and commanded the porter to watch.'

'Watch ye therefore: for ye know not when the master of the house cometh, at even, or at midnight, or at the cock-crowing, or in the morning: lest coming suddenly he find you sleeping. And what I say unto you I say unto all, Watch', Mk. 13:33-37.

Thus it was that the ascension of the Son was likened to his taking a journey, leaving a well ordered house in the care of his servants. No matter what worldly men have done in and to that house, when he returns *he will expect to find things exactly as they were when he left them.*

He has gone. And time has passed. On earth, if not yet in the heavens, the things which he said would happen in his absence have taken place, or are taking place, or will take place. Within this present age, in time, he will come back. But the day, the hour, no man knoweth.

Watch ye therefore. Watch earth. Watch heaven. Watch the passage of time. Watch the witness of the Holy Ghost. Watch the administration from the glory. Watch against the world, worldly things; worldly company; worldly religion; worldly ease and sleep. For the destiny of Christ's elect lies beyond: it lies in the world to come, whereof we speak. Amen.

IV

The Destiny of Christ and the Gospel
Chapters 14 to 16

THIS passage is not so much one of teaching; it contains the narrative of events. However, teaching cannot but be found in the arrangement and sequence of occurrences, just as it appears in Mark's inclusion or exclusion of each successive incident from this entire eventful period.

The whole sweep of the truth from Mark 14 to 16 emphasizes the momentous significance of the circumstances of Jesus' closing days. Of the two days before the passover. Of the one day. Of the final day. Of the sabbath day. And of the first day of the week, with its tremendous consequences. Here is the record of the destiny of Christ and the gospel.

Unprecedented detail crowds the evangelist's chronicle, although the period covered is little more than a few days. This format is the mind of the Spirit in Mark, and to express it, the closing events of chapter 16 are made to appear as if they followed immediately one upon another.

In order to understand the timing in Mark's account of this closing witness, it is vital to grasp the difference between Jewish daily reckoning, and that to which we are accustomed. Because the difference is considerable.

The Roman day—like our own—was measured from midnight to midnight. The Jewish day was not. By Jewish reckoning the day was counted from sunset to sunset.

This means that to the Jew the day *began* in the evening of our day, and continued throughout the night. At that midnight our day ended, and our next day began. However the Jewish day, which had begun the previous sunset, stretched throughout the night and continued beyond the dawn, encompassing both morning and afternoon, not ending till the setting of the sun. That is—as far as *we* are concerned—on the following day.

Thus the Jewish day straddled *two* of our days, and included two evenings, an entire night, a dawn, a morning, and an afternoon. Recognition of this fact immediately resolves several apparent difficulties. Lifelong familiarity with our own system of reckoning makes for awkwardness in grasping the difference between the Jewish day and our day. But it is essential to grasp the difference.

Whatever the difference, day is still day and night is still night. But *a* day differs in our reckoning from that of the Jews. A Jewish day *began* as night fell, and it did not *end* until the following nightfall. Sunset to sunset was the rule.

This simple observation explains how Christ was 'three days and three nights in the heart of the earth' after his burial, rising on the third day. Moreover it does so without resorting to contorted theories.

But that given—and it must be given—one ought not to press for chronological exactitude as to the precise number of hours involved in any one of these three days or nights. That the period took in *some* of each of the days and nights was sufficient by Jewish reckoning.

The point of the 'three days and three nights' of the burial, and of Christ's descent into the lower parts of the earth, lies in the force of Jesus' testimony, not in the minute precision of chronology. His testimony rang out with a threefold witness. He testified to the children of the day, and he testified to the children of the night.

189

In those three days, in the Spirit he witnessed in the light, and in the Spirit he witnessed in the darkness. See I Tim. 3:16; I Pet. 3:18-20; Eph. 4:9.

By the time that Christ arose bodily from the dead, that testimony to the triumph of his death had resounded from the heights of heaven to the depths of hell, for ever to divide the light from the darkness.

Thus day unto day uttereth speech, and night unto night showeth knowledge, even from the uttermost brightness of glory, to the nethermost blackness of sheol. He that hath ears to hear, let him hear.

i. Two days before the passover

Mark 14:1-11 exposes the estimation in which Christ and the gospel were held—and always would be held—in this world by various classes and conditions. The period—over the two days before the passover—reveals the destiny which sooner or later becomes inevitable, given the presence of Christ and the preaching of the gospel.

The disclosure of man's evaluation of Christ characterizes these verses. This appears consistently in the three incidents which make up the section.

First there is the estimation by the religious leaders of the truth as it is in Jesus. Just as Christ by the gospel had exposed this world's religion in the three days of his testimony at Jerusalem, so now, as passover approaches, the reaction of the religious rulers—and their unprincipled lawlessness—is brought to light.

Whether they will or not, they cannot help themselves from exposing the implacable enmity of their whole heart and soul against the truth.

'After two days was the feast of the passover, and of unleavened bread: and the chief priests and the scribes sought how they might take him by craft, and put him to death', Mk. 14:1. Their estimation of the danger he posed to themselves and their entire system resulted in the determination to put him to death.

They hated him: he was a danger to them. But they could find no fault with him, who had found such fault with them.

Was he faultless? then they must use craft. False witness; lies; slander; rumour; abuse of authority: what did it matter, so long as such a threat to their place and their religion remained? And whenever Christ and the gospel are manifested in life and power, this reaction will be inevitable. It is destiny.

'They said, Not on the feast day, lest there be an uproar of the people', Mk. 14:2. They determined upon his death, but to preserve themselves from perceived repercussions they resolved that it should not be on the feast day. Yet for all their cunning craftiness, it *was* on the feast day.

Nevertheless their hatred, fuelled by that passionate self-interest in preserving the corrupt system which gave them their place, would have amounted to nothing. Save for one factor. 'Him, *being delivered by the determinate counsel and foreknowledge of God*, ye have taken, and by wicked hands have crucified and slain', Acts 2:23.

However, to be esteemed as a sheep for the slaughter was and is the destiny of Christ and the gospel on earth at the hands of this world's religion.

That is, when once the light, life, and power of the testimony of Jesus exposes the wicked abuse of the religious leaders, and of their support for the apostasy on which they rely for their status, then—if God permit—the destiny of Christ and the gospel is sealed.

At verse three the scene changes abruptly from the palace of the high priest at Jerusalem to the house of Simon the leper in Bethany. Here Jesus is found among his own. But the way in which he is esteemed is far from uniform. Two different scales of valuation come to light, made manifest by the actions of differing parties among the disciples.

Jesus was in Bethany—the house of the poor—in the dwelling of one known as Simon the leper. What more humble condition, or what greater stigma, than that? But in this place of penury Simon gave all that he had to him from whom he had received everything. He gave his home. It was the Lord's.

Here Jesus is valued above all things. For in 'the house of the poor', and from the poorest of all, it is his destiny, and the gospel's, to find the greatest magnanimity.

As he sat at meat, there came a woman having an alabaster box of ointment of spikenard very precious; and she brake the box, and poured it on his head, Mk. 14:3.

Thereupon Jesus commented, She hath wrought a good work on me. And again he said, She hath done what she could: she is come aforehand to anoint my body to the burying.

The woman was moved in her bowels as she felt the suffering that was to fall upon Jesus; her love reached out to him because of the destiny before him. Of this he had prophesied to all. Yet their heart was hardened, as if they felt nothing of that through which Jesus was passing, and was to pass.

The woman yearned to show that she perceived; she longed to demonstrate how much she valued him; and she was moved to convey her sense of desolation because of the death that he was about to die.

But how? There was one thing that she had, and it was all that she had. She gave everything—not even the alabaster box

192

was spared—and she gave it in a gesture which revealed all that she felt. And he responded in a way which showed his awareness of everything that, mutely, she had longed to make manifest.

Jesus showed that he perceived the remarkable intuition so evidently born of the love of this un-named woman. He indicated that he recognized that she had come aforehand to anoint his body to the burying.

But the disciples showed none of this; they demonstrated nothing save heartlessness; they recognized nothing but worldly values. They had indignation against her within themselves, Mk. 14:4; accused her of waste, Mk. 14:4; murmured against her, Mk. 14:5; and troubled her, Mk. 14:6. In all this, they were wholly out of sympathy with Jesus. But she was wholly in sympathy with Jesus.

Their valuation was different. But it was—and is—his destiny that those held to be the greatest among his own should fail to understand his sufferings, and should value their own works above his person. Apparently so concerned for the poor, they counted her love but waste, Mk. 14:4,5.

Waste? So selfish about *their* good works, could they feel nothing of *the* good work—Mk. 14:6—so all-embracing to her? *Their* good works were to distribute the gifts of others upon the objects of their charity. But *her* good work was from the anguish of her heart, bestowed upon him, the love of her being. 'She hath wrought a good work on *me*', Mk. 14:6.

Nevertheless, her consolation is the greater: 'Verily I say unto you, Wheresoever this gospel' — for it is a question of Christ and the gospel — 'shall be preached throughout the whole world, this also that she hath done shall be spoken of for a memorial of her', Mk. 14:9.

Shall it? Spoken of? Have *you* ever heard this spoken of? Of all the so-called evangelists I have heard speak, and of every professed minister of the presumed gospel that has spoken in my ears, *not one* once fulfilled these words. Then how can these have preached what Christ calls 'This gospel'?

Finally, the scene changes, yet in a strange sense converges. At the palace of the high priest at Jerusalem, one of Jesus' chosen apostles came from the house of Simon the leper at Bethany. Lately he had made—if not initiated—the complaint of squandering three hundred pence, which all had judged should have been given to the poor, not 'wasted' on Jesus.

However, this apostle considers the sale of Jesus no waste, but rather gain: 'And Judas Iscariot, one of the twelve, went unto the chief priests, to betray him unto them. And when they heard it, they were glad, and promised to give him money. And he sought how he might conveniently betray him', Mk. 14:10,11.

This also is the destiny of Christ and the gospel. At the heart of the apostolate, in the midst of the apostolic ministry, 'one of the twelve' counted money to be of more worth than Jesus. Not when the possibility was non-existent. But at the last, when occasion presented itself. And if this be Jesus' destiny from one of the twelve, what can he expect from the ministry when the twelve have passed away?

ii. The day before the passover

As the second of the two days before the passover came to a close at sunset, so the great, the final day of unleavened bread, when they killed the passover, drew near with eventide. In truth, this was to be the last passover of the old testament, and with this momentous day, from even to even, would come the climax of time, the close of the legal covenant, and the end of the old creation.

'And the first day of unleavened bread, when they killed the passover, his disciples said unto him, Where wilt thou that we go and prepare that thou mayest eat the passover?', Mk. 14:12. Thus the close of the day drew on towards the evening with which the feast of unleavened bread commenced.

'And he sendeth forth two of his disciples, and saith unto them, Go ye into the city, and there shall meet you a man bearing a pitcher of water: follow him. And wheresoever he shall go in, say ye to the goodman of the house, The Master saith, Where is the guestchamber, where I shall eat the passover with my disciples?'.

'And he will show you a large upper room furnished and prepared: there make ready for us. And his disciples went forth, and came into the city, and found as he had said unto them: and they made ready the passover', Mk. 14:13-16.

Only Mark and Luke write of the mystery of the man bearing the pitcher of water, Luke adding the names of the two disciples —Peter and John—sent to intercept his passing as they entered the gates of Jerusalem. All this was divine; Jesus did not arrange it: he saw into heaven, and thus into the future, and foretold what would come to pass.

And so it was. At this the last passover of the covenant; at this the conclusion of the old testament; at this the beginning of the day — from even to even — at the close of which Jesus would be crucified, dead, and buried: the two disciples went forth into the city to prepare the passover.

All the prophets of the old covenant come to a point in their testimony; all the scriptures of the law and the prophets merge together in their witness: just as the entry of the two disciples through the gates of the city coincided precisely with the passing of the man bearing the pitcher of water.

Of water? 'But this spake he of the Spirit, which they that believe on him should receive.' Water? Here is a symbol of the Holy Ghost. The Spirit came upon all the prophets which have been since the world began, up to and including John the Baptist. As one they pointed to Christ. As one they prophesied of that which was beyond all conception, the coming of the new testament.

The Spirit came upon the prophets, yes, and of this the mysterious figure of the man *bearing* the pitcher of water witnessed. But in the new testament the Spirit which was then *with* them should dwell *in* them. 'Shall be *in him* a well of water springing up into everlasting life.' 'Out of his *belly* shall flow rivers of living water.'

Every prophecy, all scripture, the entire testimony of the saints of the old testament, everything led up to the glory of the coming of Christ and the new testament. Every word, every direction of the Holy Ghost converged to witness of the coming of the apostle and mediator who should bring in the new covenant. 'When Christ cometh, he shall tell us all things.'

Salvation was of the Jews. 'Our feet shall stand within thy gates, O Jerusalem.' And as the feet of Peter and John stood within those gates, *at that precise moment* there passed the man bearing a pitcher of water. They followed him. He led to a destination they could not have found without him. Passing through the gates of the house, the man to whom they had never spoken disappeared from their view.

They stood at the open door, waiting. The goodman of the house knew them, who knew not him. Expecting them, he led them up to a large upper—the wording is literally 'above the earth'—room, furnished and prepared.

They had been directed to the city; led to the house; conducted to that heavenly room. Here, in a figure, the old would pass away, and the new would be ushered in.

In this upper, heavenly, room; in this large place; in this dwelling furnished with all the spiritual substance which the shadowy furniture of the tabernacle had prefigured, that is, every divine provision for the whole new testament throughout the entire age, here, I say, the final passover was to be concluded. And Christ our passover was to be foreshadowed as sacrificed for us in the last supper.

iii. *The passover*

'And in the evening'—the beginning of the Jewish day—'he cometh with the twelve.' That is, to eat the passover. And as they ate, he prophesied, saying that one of them should betray him.

Then began they to be sorrowful. However, their sorrow was not from sympathy that he should be betrayed, but lest they personally should be the betrayer. 'They say unto him *one by one*, Is it I? and another said, Is it I?'. Here 'I' is central, not 'thou'.

Nevertheless, they were central to him: 'And as they did eat, Jesus took bread, and blessed, and brake it, and gave to them, and said, Take, eat: this is my body.'

'And he took the cup, and when he had given thanks, he gave it to them: and they all drank of it. And he said unto them, This is my blood of the new testament, which is shed for many', Mk. 14:22-24.

There is no question in this place of repeating the enactment of the supper. Nothing whatsoever is said here of *their* doing this in memory of him. In Mark it is solely a graphic picture of what *he* should do for *them*. Of his giving his body and blood for the 'many'. Of this sacrifice they should partake in a mystery. This is what the supper depicts in Mark.

And when they had sung an hymn, they went out into the mount of Olives. The night had closed in round about them. As they went, Jesus prophesied once more: 'All ye shall be offended because of me this night.' Likewise he foretold of his being smitten, and of his rising again.

Peter ignored the things which Jesus said about himself—*such* things!—and, taking personal offence, protested that *he* would never be offended because of Jesus. But Jesus prophesied that 'this day'—mark that, this *day*—'even in this night, before the cock crow twice, thou shalt deny me thrice', Mk. 14:30.

Peter the more vehemently contradicted Jesus. He would *never* deny him. And likewise said they all. Had they dwelt more on *him*, and forgotten *themselves*, they might have known that his prophecy was certain, and, however sorrowful over their own frailty, might have found room for sympathy, and time to comfort.

But this loneliness of heart was his—and it is the gospel's— destiny on earth, suffered even from his own.

And they came to a place which was named Gethsemane, and he said to his disciples, Sit ye here, while I shall pray. And he taketh with him Peter, and James, and John, and began to be sore amazed, and very heavy: and he said unto them, My soul is exceeding sorrowful unto death: tarry ye here, and watch, Mk. 14:32-34.

Watch: 'Behold, and see if there be any sorrow like unto my sorrow.' He is a man of sorrows, and acquainted with grief. Watch. Whilst, 'The sorrows of death compassed me.' When,

'The sorrows of hell compassed me about: the snares of death prevented me.' But what of sympathy from the disciples?

Wherefore he saith, 'Reproach hath broken my heart; and I am full of heaviness: and I looked for some to take pity, but there was none; and for comforters, but I found none.' 'I looked on my right hand, and beheld, but there was no man that would know me: refuge failed me; no man cared for my soul.' Said he, 'I have trodden the winepress alone.'

'And he went forward a little, and fell on the ground', Mk. 14:35. Matthew tells us 'he fell on his face', Mt. 26:39; and Luke, that 'he kneeled down, and prayed'. Again, 'And being in an agony he prayed more earnestly: and his sweat was as it were great drops of blood falling to the ground', Luke 22:41-44.

To this Hebrews refers, saying, Who in the days of his flesh, when he had offered up prayers and supplications with strong crying and tears unto him that was able to save him from death, was heard in that he feared. Though he were a Son, yet learned he obedience by the things which he suffered, Heb. 5:7,8. This also is the destiny of Christ and the gospel.

Three times he prayed. Three times he came back to Peter, James, and John. The first time, 'he cometh and findeth them sleeping, and saith unto Peter, Simon, sleepest thou? couldest not thou watch one hour?' This was the first hour.

And again he went away and prayed. And when he returned, he found them asleep again (for their eyes were heavy,) neither wist they what to answer him. This was the next hour.

And he cometh the third time. This time his prayers were concluded. It was the final hour. The matter was settled. 'Sleep on now, and take your rest.'

His being sore amazed; his being very heavy; his soul being exceeding sorrowful even unto death: these were things unique to him. But because the spiritual powers of darkness closed in all around, this affected them. It was not sleep in and of itself: it was the *sheer weight* of the forces which compassed him about, that the disciples found too exhausting to bear. They were drained beyond measure.

It was dark. But it was more than dark. 'This is your hour, and the *power* of darkness', Luke 22:53. There bowed down upon him '*the rulers* of the darkness of this world', the 'spiritual wickedness in heavenly places', Eph. 6:12.

The prince of this world, the prince of darkness, returning with redoubled malevolence, made the darkness palpable, vibrant with evil power. 'The prince of this world cometh', Jesus had said, 'and hath nothing in me', John 14:30.

Upon his knees; upon the ground; upon his face; sweating as it were great drops of blood: his prayers prevailed. Two words are used to describe his prayers. One means 'Beseeching prayer, supplication'; the root of which indicates 'to be in want; in need to ask; to beseech'. The other word occurs but once in the new testament, meaning, literally, 'for intensity of pleading'.

Withal such prayer these three times, we are told of his 'being in an agony'; of his 'strong'— or robust—'crying'. The Greek word for crying has been used to convey the baying of dogs; the croaking of frogs; screaming; and the shouting of men. This gives force to the words 'strong crying and tears'.

Sweat as great drops of blood; agony; *strong* crying; falling upon his face; and, he was heard in that 'he feared'. This marks the scene of his being sore amazed; very heavy; sorrowful unto death; crying aloud, as, prostrate in the dust, he agonized alone in prayer at Gethsemane.

Apart from the assault of the prince and the powers of darkness that closed in about him, of far greater moment was his agony over the cup. It was over what was *before* him, not what was immediate to him. The prospect of the cup came with a dread that was unprecedented.

Here was the Son of God from eternity crying to his Father in the frailty of his human nature. Three times he said it: 'Abba, Father, all things are possible unto thee; take away this cup from me: nevertheless not what I will, but what thou wilt.'

It was not that he had drunk of the cup. But now, at the end, in this last hour, the Father presented the cup to Jesus' conscious awareness in a way that was without precedent. He would not, he could not, drink the contents till on the cross and at the place of atonement. But he could, and he did, look into those contents at the place called Gethsemane. And the powers of darkness fell upon him as he did so.

Three times he prayed: *'Take away this cup from me.'* Three times there was silence. After the third occasion, *still* the Father had not answered. But the Son had been heard. Silence. That *was* the answer.

Submissive, he took the cup, not from Israel, not from Rome, much less the darkness that filled his murderers: he took the cup from his Father. To him there were no second causes. Just as to him the silence had testified to the answer three times over.

He took; he submitted; he received the cup. On the cross, in the hours of substitutionary atonement, it would be brought to and tilted at his lips, and he would drink it to the dregs. No one would see, nor could any see, this divine enactment which would be at once invisible, mysterious, and spiritual. Nor could any comprehend the absolute enormity of what he should drink down into his inmost soul.

'Who his own self bare our sins in his own body on the tree', I Pet. 2:24. 'The LORD hath laid on him the iniquity of us all', Isa. 53:6. 'For he hath made him to be sin for us, who knew no sin', II Cor. 5:21. Who knew no sin; who did no sin; who was without sin.

The cup, drained, meant that he should know sin: our sin; that he should be made sin: made sin for us. It meant that all our iniquity was laid upon him, as if it were his: as if *he* had done it; the imbibing of the cup meant *interior conscious contact* with that which was beyond horror to his spotless soul.

This was that which caused him to agonize; to cry; to sweat; to weep: 'Take away *this* cup from me.' But the silence was his answer. For his Father; for us sinners; there was no alternative. And, spiritually, he reached out in the meekness of his obedient submission. He reached out, and took the cup.

There on the cross, having drunk in the contents, being made one with his people in their sin and on their behalf, the Substitute of sinners hung. But this was not all. Having first borne the sin, it must follow that he should suffer the punishment.

He must needs suffer under the curse of the law; he must needs bear the rigorous stripes of the rod of legal justice; he must needs agonize under the eternal wrath of God; he must needs be borne down beneath the judgment of everlasting divine righteousness: these things also were in the cup which he drained at the cross.

Well might his people sleep on now, and take their rest. For he would do all, who required nothing, that he might finish the work which his Father had given him to do. And this was no more than he had said: 'Nevertheless not what I will, but what thou wilt.'

Now events crowd swiftly one upon another, hastening through the night and the following day, that is, towards the next evening which would conclude the first day of unleavened bread. This is that same day on the *previous* evening of which the passover had been killed and eaten.

Then said Jesus, The hour is come; behold, the Son of man is betrayed into the hands of sinners. Rise up, let us go; lo, he that betrayeth me is at hand.

And immediately, while he yet spake, cometh Judas, one of the twelve, and with him a great multitude with swords and staves, from the chief priests and the scribes and the elders.

And he that betrayed him had given them a token, saying, Whomsoever I shall kiss, the same is he; take him and lead him away safely.

And as soon as he was come, he goeth straightway to him, and saith, Master, master; and kissed him. Now this is the destiny of Christ and the gospel, nor can either fare otherwise in this present world. But the worst of it is that this betrayal to the waiting hierarchy came from the very centre of his own chosen ministers: 'one of the twelve.'

Laying hands on Jesus, they took him. The ineffectual use of a sword availed nothing. Jesus protested against the surreptitious behaviour of those sent unlawfully in the night from the chief priests, scribes, and elders. But, he concluded, 'the scriptures must be fulfilled', Mk. 14:49.

Then all forsook him and fled, who the same night in which he was betrayed had indignantly protested their undying fidelity.

The young man who followed him likewise fled naked, rather leaving his flimsy covering than be taken captive with Jesus. And what was he, but a figure of them all? But this is the destiny of Christ and the gospel, and, worst, at the hands of his own in the hour of his extremity.

To suffer his destiny — with that of his gospel — from this world's religion, Jesus is led away to the high priest and the entire assembly of the elders and the scribes. Peter followed afar off, entering into the palace of the high priest, and, with great courage, seated himself with the servants about the fire.

The chief priests and all the council laboured throughout that night to create appearances which would justify their lawless and unjust condemnation, a condemnation determined not simply *when* Jesus was brought before them, but *two days* previously, Mk. 14:1,2.

Where was the legality, let alone the justice, of such proceedings, in which the judge first pronounced the verdict, then laboured mightily through the darkness of the night to fabricate some sort of makeshift evidence to justify the sentence already passed?

'And the chief priests and all the council *sought* for witness against Jesus to put him to death.'

But the only legal ground of passing sentence of death lay in a proper court of law duly convened, first to hear and try the evidence of witnesses summoned before and examined by the court, *then* to pass judgment. But the chief priests and all the council of the Jews were different. They condemned first, and sought for witnesses afterwards.

'They sought for witness against Jesus to put him to death; *and found none*', Mk. 14:55. Nevertheless they did discover something: 'Many bare false witness against him, but their witness agreed not together', Mk. 14:56. If not, no case existed, since two or three witnesses were imperative for conviction under the law.

Hence the religious authorities laboured long and hard through the night, rousing one after another from their beds to lend their assistance to a murder decided long before the perjurers blundered their way through the darkness to the unlawfully called assembly. 'And there arose certain'—at last— 'but neither so did their witness agree together', Mk. 14:57,59.

Beside himself with frustration, the high priest stood up in the midst, and demanded of Jesus — who had maintained a composed silence throughout the proceedings — Answerest thou nothing? what is it which these witness against thee? But Jesus continued to hold his peace.

'Again the high priest asked him, and said unto him, Art thou the Christ, the Son of the Blessed?' But why ask that? Because *that* was the reason for the premeditated murder. Jesus' silence had forced the issue, bringing the high priest to ask the question which gave him away, together with all those who had determined that death was the only possible destiny for Christ and the gospel.

'And Jesus said, I am: and ye shall see the Son of man sitting on the right hand of power, and coming in the clouds of heaven', Mk. 14:62. This was no more than the truth. And for that truth, this world's religion—which had long determined to stamp out both him and his gospel—now foisted their murderous intentions upon the trumped-up charge of blasphemy.

'The high priest rent his clothes, and saith, What need we any further witnesses?' *Further* witnesses? They had not found so much as one witness.

'Ye have heard the blasphemy.' No. They had heard the truth, as they well knew, and would know in the resurrection of damnation when the Son of man should come again in his glory. 'What think ye? And they all condemned him to be guilty of death', Mk. 14:64.

And some began to spit on him, and to cover his face, and to buffet him, and to say unto him, Prophesy: and the servants did strike him with the palms of their hands. But this was his destiny from religion on earth, and as a sheep before her shearers is dumb, so he opened not his mouth. He gave his back to the smiters, and his cheeks to them that plucked out the hair.

Now Mark unexpectedly shifts the scene, interweaving a minor theme with the main narrative. The remainder of the chapter focusses on Peter, who stood beneath in the palace.

No one should minimize the bravery of Peter, nor mistake his ardent devotion. Peter's tragic discovery, however, was that for all his determination not to deny Jesus, the flesh was helpless before the powers of darkness, nor could what was carnal attain to things that were spiritual.

The downfall of the courageous Peter came about because of two precocious, tongue-wagging, and mischief-making young females, both mere maids. Nothing could quieten them, for, in truth—and in turn—the demons had agitated their fleshly propensities and inflated their self-importance.

Thus Satan prepared his sieve to sift Peter, and, he hoped, utterly to destroy his faith, bringing him down to despair and death.

Came the first, boldly staring at Peter, excited by her discovery: 'And thou also wast with Jesus of Nazareth'! To avoid the maid's blazing abroad her suspicions, Peter professed ignorance.

He denied it, saying, 'I know not, neither understand I what thou sayest.' Knowing that neither his denial nor anything else would still the tongue of such a female, Peter removed himself, going out into the porch. And the cock crew. As yet this did not register in Peter's mind. What registered was the hope that by such evasive action, he might remain as near to Jesus as possible.

But Satan had not yet done: he had only begun. Came the second maid, equally agitated and officious, pointing the finger at Peter, as she began to shrill her tirade to those that stood by, 'This is one of them'! And he denied it again.

But by now the harm was done, and suspicion had been sown. A little after, they that stood by said again to Peter, Surely thou *art* one of them. Peter began to curse and to swear, saying, I know not this man of whom ye speak. For at all costs, to his very life, he was determined to abide by Jesus. But the second time the cock crew, Mk. 14:72.

And Peter called to mind the word that Jesus had said unto him, Before the cock crow twice, thou shalt deny me thrice. And when he thought thereon, he wept. With all his spirit he had tried; and with all his flesh he had failed.

Nevertheless Jesus had said beforehand — though not in Mark—'Simon, Simon, behold, Satan hath desired to have you, that he may sift you as wheat: but I have prayed for thee, that thy faith fail not: and when thou art converted, strengthen thy brethren.' This should come to pass, when Christ was glorified, the Spirit was given, and when the gospel prevailed.

And straightway in the morning—that is, at sunrise on *the same Jewish day* as that which had commenced at the previous sunset and would not end until the following sunset—the chief priests held a consultation with the elders and scribes and the whole council.

But why consult on what they had resolved? Because they must decide how to present their resolution to murder Jesus in terms acceptable to the Roman governor, who, perforce, must execute the sentence. What sentence? The unjust condemnation passed at an unlawful assembly, for no cause other than that he *was* the Christ, the Son of the Blessed.

They held a consultation. How should they put this to Pilate? They bound Jesus, and carried him away, and delivered him to the governor. And Pilate asked him, Art thou the King of the Jews? But why ask that? Because it was the deceitful charge laid before Pilate after their consultation, clean contrary to that for which they themselves had sentenced him earlier that night.

But this was, is, and always will be, the nature of this world's religion, epitomized in the hierarchical body that, with the 'scholars' and elders, will ever appear as its head. It was, is, and must be so, because its spirit and genius is that of the god of this world, the father of lies, who abode not in the truth. Just so these told—and tell—lies from the beginning.

Said Pilate, 'Art thou the King of the Jews?' Jesus answered, 'Thou sayest it.' That is, Not me. He did not say it. The Jews said it. And they said this because it was a capital offence, directly challenging the authority of Caesar. Pilate asked if this were true, but Jesus' answer was that the governor had said it, not him. Jesus had not said it, nor did he say it then.

At this the chief priests took alarm, lest their scheming plot should fail. Losing all control, they take to clamour, 'Accusing him of many things', Mk. 15:3. But he answered nothing.

Pilate asked him again, 'Answerest thou nothing? behold how many things they witness against thee'! Yes, because their carefully crafted accusation adapted to the ears of the governor had been neatly countered by Jesus' reply. Hence the tumult of those who cared only to have him put to death, and not at all under which accusation this should come to pass.

But Jesus yet answered nothing, so that Pilate marvelled. For by now this man of the world had seen through this world's religion, even as he saw through the intentions of its leaders.

But to no avail. Pilate attempted a face-saving compromise, appealing to the Roman governor's custom of releasing at that feast one prisoner, no matter his crimes. To do so would—Pilate hoped—satisfy the religious rulers, in that such a pardon would at once justify them in their accusations, and him in his just desire to acquit the prisoner.

'For he knew that the chief priests had delivered him for envy.' But he was worse off for his attempt to save Jesus, since his compromise required him to admit that the prisoner was guilty. Sensing their opportunity, the chief priests moved the multitude, by now in a frenzy, so that the entire Jewish people cried out for Jesus to be crucified.

Alarmed at the ferocity of the uproar, Pilate, willing—more than willing: matters were out of control; Pilate was forced by events—to content the people, released Barabbas unto them, and delivered Jesus, when he had scourged him, to be crucified. And this was Jesus' destiny, and that of the gospel, in this world, both from it, and from its religion.

The soldiers led Jesus away, and, calling the whole band, clothed him with purple, and put a crown of thorns upon his head. They mocked him, saluting him, and saying, Hail, King of the Jews. They smote him with a reed, spitting upon him, and bowing their knees, derided him with mock obeisance.

When they had concluded their ridicule, they took off the purple from him, and putting his own clothes on him, led him out to crucify him. Seeing one that passed by, they compelled him to bear his cross. But why? This almost certainly indicates the exhaustion of Jesus, to which the long night, and terrible morning, together with the scourging and mocking, had reduced him.

And they bring him unto the place Golgotha, which is, being interpreted, The place of a skull. And they gave him to drink wine mingled with myrrh: but he received it not. And when they had crucified him, they parted his garments, passing lots upon them, what every man should take.

And it was the third hour, and they crucified him. This was nine o'clock in the morning.

Two thieves were crucified with him, the one on his right hand, the other on his left. Mark observes, 'And the scripture was fulfilled, which saith, And he was numbered with the transgressors', Mk. 15:28.

For three hours Jesus hung on the cross in full daylight, until twelve noon, a witness to all time of the destiny meted out by this world, and by worldly religion, to Christ and his gospel.

During these three hours of daylight three classes of persons manifested the implacable unbelief and adamant hardness of heart of carnal and worldly religion against the mediator and apostle of the new testament.

First there were those that passed by. Next there were the chief priests with the scribes. Finally there were those crucified with him. The first railed on him. The next mocked at him. And the last reviled him.

The passers-by railed on him, wagging their heads, taunting him by repeating the contradictions of witnesses so false that even the chief priests and scribes had rejected them. The passers-by called on him to save himself, and come down from the cross. But he had suffered being nailed to the cross to save those that passed by. How should he then come down from the cross?

Likewise also the chief priests mocking said among themselves with the scribes, He saved others; himself he cannot save. Not so. Himself he *would* not save, *because* he was saving others. Saving them not now for time, from diseases, through his life. But saving them for eternity, from sin and wrath, by his death.

They mocked on, 'Let Christ the King of Israel descend now from the cross, that we may see and believe.' But if he did—for he could—descend from the cross there would not *be* anything to believe. For what must be believed, is that which was wrought on the cross.

And they that were crucified with him, in the midst of their long-drawn-out death throes, reviled him for saving neither himself nor them. But his salvation was eternal, not temporal. It was through death, not out of it. It was for the world to come, not for the world that now is.

And when the sixth hour—that is, twelve noon—was come, there was darkness over the whole land until the ninth hour, Mk. 15:33. What should now pass between the Father and the Son would reach into the eternal; the infinite; the absolute: it lay in a darkness beyond human penetration.

This was the *mystery* of the gospel: at once divine, heavenly, spiritual, eternal, and invisible. Eye could not see, nor ear hear, nor could it enter into the heart of man to conceive the length, the breadth, the depth, the height, of the invisible transaction that took place in the darkness.

Christ should now finish the transgression, make an end of sins, make reconciliation for iniquity, and bring in everlasting righteousness. He would lift the cup to his lips, draining its contents into his own body, withal bearing the everlasting punishment of a people whose number exceeded the stars in the sky for multitude, and the sand which is by the sea-shore innumerable.

No eye saw it. No flesh understood it. No man knew it. Only God Almighty in the heavens, and that frail humanity upon the cross, conceived the profound mystery of this, the day of atonement. The world's religion was oblivious to it. The world was ignorant of it. And of this blind obscurity, the three hours darkness bore mute testimony.

And at the ninth hour—three in the afternoon—Jesus cried with a loud voice, Eloi, Eloi, lama sabachthani? which is, being interpreted, My God, my God, why hast thou forsaken me? Why had God forsaken him? He was forsaken because of the sins of his people, removed from them and borne by Jesus in his own body on the tree. He was cut off because God had made him to be sin for us, that it might be condemned in his flesh on our behalf.

The wrath of God then having fallen out of eternity upon the sin-bearer on the cross, God having been glorified in righteousness by the judgment of sins in the Substitute, what remained? The blind ignorance and superstition of man remained, so foolish as to suppose Jesus would call upon the saints, confounding 'Eloi' with 'Elias'.

And Jesus cried with a loud voice, and gave up the ghost. It was finished. The cup was empty. The will of God was accomplished. And the new testament was immutably established on an indestructible basis which would abide for ever, world without end. Amen.

And the veil of the temple was rent in twain from the top to the bottom: 'he taketh away the first, that he may establish the second.' Of which the rent veil bore witness. The old covenant, with its worldly sanctuary, earthly temple, legal dispensation, and carnal priesthood, passed away with the rending of the veil, never to return again. 'From the top to the bottom', Mk. 15:38.

'And when the centurion, which stood over against him, saw that he so cried out, and gave up the ghost, he said, Truly this man was the Son of God', Mk. 15:39. The centurion *saw* that he cried out? Did he not rather *hear?* Doubtless he heard.

But there was that about the way in which Jesus cried out that was expressive of such divinity, and that about the way in which he expired that manifest so great a triumph, that the centurion—it was not so much what he heard—saw in this that which caused him to confess, 'Truly this man was the Son of God'.

There were also women looking on afar off: among whom was Mary Magdalene, and Mary the mother of James the less and of Joses, and Salome; (who also, when he was in Galilee, followed him, and ministered unto him;) and many other women, which came up with him unto Jerusalem.

First the Gentile centurion, who was so impressed with the manner of Jesus' death that he could do no other than confess him to be the Son of God. Then many faithful women, some known for their ministry to him, but every one godly, and each a long-time follower of Jesus from the days in Galilee.

These all witnessed the end. It was about three in the afternoon. This was still the first day of unleavened bread, on the previous evening of which they had slain the passover. That day was not yet over.

And now, when the even was come—or rather, more strictly, as the afternoon began to draw to a close—because it was the preparation, that is, the day before the sabbath, Joseph of Arimathaea, an honourable counsellor, which also waited for the kingdom of God, came, and went in boldly unto Pilate, and craved the body of Jesus.

Momentous as was that feast day, as it drew to a conclusion other considerations pressed in upon the Jews. It was the day before the sabbath, when no work of any kind might be done.

Hence the intense activity as the evening drew on: for everything must be prepared, so that, as sunset fell, all work was wrought in advance, ready against the hours of the sabbath.

Urgent in the mind of Joseph was the burial of Jesus, of necessity before sunset. He must be buried on *that* day. He could not be buried on the sabbath day. Hence—as the afternoon sun began to sink—the urgency of Joseph's activity.

And Pilate marvelled if Jesus were already dead: and calling unto him the centurion, he asked him whether he had been any while dead. And when he knew it of the centurion—the same that had seen when Jesus so cried out, and gave up the ghost, at about three that afternoon—Pilate gave the body to Joseph.

Joseph bought fine linen, and took Jesus down, and wrapped him in the linen. John tells us that Nicodemus accompanied Joseph, but this is not recorded by Mark, who states simply that Joseph laid the body of Jesus in a sepulchre which was hewn out of a rock, and rolled a stone unto the door of the sepulchre.

And Mary Magdalene and Mary the mother of Joses beheld where Jesus' body was laid. Albeit late, this was still the afternoon—drawing on towards the setting of the sun—of the sixth day, namely, the first day of unleavened bread and of the passover. However, late or not, Luke assures us that the women still had time to return and prepare spices and ointments before the Jewish day had ended.

iv. The sabbath day

The moment the sun set below the horizon, all work ceased. The sabbath day had commenced. Then, Luke tells us of the women 'They rested the sabbath day according to the commandment', Lk. 23:56.

However, in view of the activity of the women *after* the burial of Jesus' body — he having died at three that afternoon — it becomes obvious that Jesus was both dead and buried well before sunset ushered in that sabbath. And, indeed, this was his destiny, for so it is written in the scriptures.

v. The first day

The last chapter of Mark selectively records the events of the first day of the week, beginning with the vision of the young man in the sepulchre, where the body of Jesus had lain, Mk. 16:1-8.

The young man, sitting on the right side, clothed in a long white garment, appeared within the tomb to Mary Magdalene, Mary the mother of James, and Salome. Here is a resurrection vision, and it is made manifest to devout women.

The visionary young man appears in the very place from which the Lord arose from the dead: 'He is risen; he is not here: behold the place where they laid him.'

The vision shows that, from the resurrection, Jesus' same apostolic life and power are perpetuated on earth in those apostolic ministers sent from heaven throughout his absence from this scene.

This is perceived by the young man's presence in the place which the risen Son had vacated. Such a visionary revelation opens the truth that Christ sends one—yes, one; the vision is of one—to continue, to recover, to restore, to revive, and to reform that which was from the beginning, even to the end of time.

The heavenly vision is certain, it shall be fulfilled, so long as the age shall last. This is manifested by the appearance of the young man seated in the place where Christ crucified had lain in death, and whence he arose from the dead.

The seated young man in the vision answers to the ministry of the new testament from the glory to the end of time. The Acts of the Apostles records the immediate fulfilment of the vision, first in Peter, then in Paul, both of whom manifested the supernatural power of the apostolic witness to Christ's resurrection, just as did John at the last.

This *is* the ministry of the new testament. The first had waxed old; it had perished; it had passed away for ever. Moses had disappeared from view. Sinai was the 'old' mount, answering to the old covenant, which did nothing but gender to bondage.

The law, the curse, the old testament: these things lay on *this* side of death, and could not pass from thence to the realm of life in the Spirit in the new testament, secured by the resurrection of Jesus Christ from the dead.

Hence Mark 16:1 opens by signifying this momentous deliverance from the old covenant, from the ancient bondage, and, indeed, from the past creation. Mark does not *begin* by saying 'On the first day of the week'. He shows the perpetuity of the new testament, established by the resurrection of the first begotten from the dead, by beginning with the assurance that 'the *sabbath* was *past*', Mk. 16:1.

The new covenant of grace, so soon to be promulgated from heavenly mount Zion by the apostle of our profession, risen from the dead, appears in the vision on the first day unveiled to the undying devotion of three women. It was revealed to the meek and broken in heart, to the intuitive insight of love. This appears in the threefold feminine witness.

Carnal reason, scholastic study, intellectual inquiry, rational deduction: these things have no place in this vision. Such things do not *appear* here, nor are *they* apparent in those at the tomb. Moreover, even if the carnal mind of man were *able* to enter and intrude, nothing would appear to that quarter but emptiness and confusion. And so it has proved—especially with the closing verses of Mark—in the issue.

On the part of man—even of the disciples—not only the first eight verses but virtually the whole of the chapter presents a catalogue of grief, misery, unbelief, and hardness of heart. The women came to anoint Jesus, yes; it is their tender and touching solicitude, surely: but they *expect* him *still* to be dead. What? After all that he had foretold of the resurrection on the third day?

They come to the tomb, they are drawn from the depths of the affection of their hearts, certainly. But they do not *expect* to be able to enter into the sepulchre. They do not *expect* to be able to embalm the dead body which they are convinced lies cold in death beyond the sealed entrance. 'Who shall roll us away the stone from the door of the sepulchre?', Mk. 16:3.

But the stone *was* rolled away. And the body was *gone*. In place of what they *expected*, once in the tomb, they saw the heavenly vision. The revelation of the new, the everlasting covenant broke forth before their wondering eyes. Yes, but for all this, 'they trembled and were amazed'.

The visionary young man in the tomb at the rising of the sun on the first day of the week announced the glorious resurrection: he commanded them to tell Jesus' disciples, and Peter, that the risen Lord went before them into Galilee. But the women say nothing at all. They tell nobody. Not a word to Peter. Why not? 'For they were afraid', Mk. 16:8.

In fact this miserable reaction made no difference. The whole chapter vibrates with the Lord's ascendancy over all their grief; misery; unbelief; and hardness of heart. He overcame all, triumphed above everything, and swept aside each one of their petty limitations as if these did not exist.

Had they come to anoint the dead body? But, 'He is risen; he is not here: behold the place where they laid him.' It was the place from which God had already raised him from the dead. 'As he said unto you.' Who shall roll us away the stone? 'When they looked, the stone *was* rolled away.' Tell his disciples? But they were afraid. But all this made no difference.

Their fear; their grief; their unbelief; their hardness of heart: these things simply did not count. They made no difference. It was the Lord that made the difference. He who rose over all, overcame all. In his disciples.

In glorious majesty the mediator and apostle of the new testament soared above their limitations. Shaming them, yes, —for there could be no room for the flesh—but withal lifting his elect, for whom he died, over all in himself, by his own resurrection life and power.

This sovereign initiative of the Son of God in putting forth his irresistible and almighty strength came *after* the fullest possible exhibition of the disciples' despondency, hopelessness, failure, and unbelief. In the end, I say, all this made no difference: he overcame all, and overcame all *in them*, at last to establish in their hearts the faith of God's elect.

Following the vision of the young man to the three women in the tomb, Mk. 16:1-8, Jesus himself appeared first to Mary Magdalene, who was disbelieved by those that had been with him; next to two of them, whom the residue likewise doubted; and finally to the eleven, Mk. 16:9-20.

But these verses — the last twelve verses of Mark — are disputed. However, they cry out to us with a loud voice, 'Do thyself no harm: for we are all here'.

Those who are under the anointing know that the Spirit of truth bears incontestable witness to these verses. Those who hear the voice of the Son of God speaking from heaven know that he who is the truth gives clear apostolic testimony to these verses.

And those who dwell in him who has been our habitation in all generations know that the God of truth has glorified his Son Jesus, precisely as recorded in the last twelve verses of Mark. For this glory is his destiny.

Others, who think that they can arrive at such a conviction by way of reasoning, when it is given to the saints by way of revelation, will find at the last that nothing but frustration awaits their endeavour. These persons have turned to the wrong quarter, and have condemned themselves to wander through an endless maze of confusing darkness.

God frustrateth the tokens of the liars, and maketh diviners mad; he turneth wise men backwards, and maketh their knowledge foolish. Where is the wise? Where is the scribe? Where is the disputer of this world? Hath not God made foolish the wisdom of this world? For it is written, I will destroy the wisdom of the wise, and bring to nothing the understanding of the prudent.

Whoso seeks to overturn this divine counsel, enquiring at the mouth of scholars and diviners, and from the wise and prudent in religion, shall find that God is well able to send them strong delusion, that they should believe a lie.

Nevertheless if they insist upon the process of reason to guide them—but it will do them no good: because the rationale of religious education is no substitute for the anointing which teacheth us all things, I John 2:27—I say, if they will trust in the equity of reason to guide them past the lies of disputers, they should turn to Dean Burgon's 'The Last Twelve Verses of Mark'.

When published in 1871, this honest and painstaking work devastated the flimsy pretexts upon which contemporary critics had revived the ancient and centuries-dormant lacerations of the four gospels by certain of the so-called 'fathers'.

These 'fathers', obsessed with amalgamating the gospels, had no scruple in dismissing what they could not 'harmonize'. Nor did they hesitate to truncate the last twelve verses of Mark to aid the hand-tooled fabrication of their monstrous 'harmony'. But Burgon's work exposed this age-old wickedness in a way that was and is unanswerable.

With able scholarship Dean Burgon demonstrated in his day that the ancient schemes of these so-called 'fathers' to rend Mark 16 — schemes rejected over the intervening centuries — survived in but *one or two* older manuscript *copies*, extant only because despised and forgotten. And in these mouldy and tasteless crumbs—'some ancient authorities' indeed!—lay the origin of 'disputing' the last twelve verses of Mark.

I say, Burgon's work was and is unanswerable; because no critic—so-called—from that day to this has found it possible to refute the Dean's invincible arguments in favour of the last twelve verses of Mark.

However, by this time commercial interests had dictated that the critics must ignore Burgon—not to mention Dr. Scrivener— against their own consciences. Nevertheless the man had for ever shattered the illusion, based upon godless and irrational theorizing, which blasphemously proposed to butcher the last chapter of the beginning of the gospel of Jesus Christ, the Son of God.

The publishers — backed by vested interests — had scented money in 1881, with the lucrative prospect of the opening of the floodgates to innumerable versions in consequence. And so it has come to pass.

Burgon might be right; he was right: but what had that to do with the chief priests, the scribes, and the elders, in view of their advantageous alliance with the traders in the outer court? To them, *money* talks. And *that* is the reason—and, after Burgon's work, left without excuse, the *only* reason—for the turning of centuries of fidelity to the text, into infidelity.

Nevertheless, by the Spirit of my God, and in the name of the Lord Jesus, I testify plainly to all who forsake the divinely-owned bible of our fathers, in favour of the increasing decadence of the modern versions — either casting doubt on, or actually obliterating, Mk. 16:9-20 — that they are under a blinding delusion.

And no amount of protestation against the trifling few corrections by which the Authorized Version might have benefited can alter these solid facts to which the Holy Ghost bears witness. He that hath an ear, let him hear what the Spirit saith.

The Spirit will not support that which annihilates his own word. He is the Spirit of truth. Those who believe a lie will never have his witness in any one part of those commercial exploitations to which the publishers have brazenly transferred the title 'bible'.

'Bible'? That which would rob Christ of *one* of the *only two* records of the ascension in the gospels? 'Bible'? That which would erase the very words of God? 'Bible'? That which would wrest the sword of the Spirit out of his own hands?

The truth is that Mark *does* conclude his gospel with the threefold testimony to the resurrection of Christ from the dead. First he appeared to Mary Magdalene; next he appeared in another form to two of them as they walked in the country; and last he appeared unto the eleven as they sat at meat.

Here is a triple witness to the bodily resurrection of Jesus from the dead. When it is said that God raised him from the

221

dead, there is nothing transient or ephemeral about this: resurrection *refers* to the body. It is *this* to which the appearances of Jesus witness. It is no gospel that ends without the resurrection *of the body*.

However, the evil heart of unbelief common to man, and incapable of faith, manifested itself with equal force in the disciples when they heard that Jesus was risen from the dead. Had not the power of Christ overcome this otherwise incurable propensity of the heart, no flesh should have been saved.

He appeared first to Mary Magdalene, out of whom he had cast seven devils. She went and told them that had been with him. And they, when they heard that he had been seen of her, 'believed not', Mk. 16:11.

Then he appeared in another form to two of them as they walked, and went into the country. They went and told it unto the residue. 'Neither believed they them', Mk. 16:13.

Finally, he appeared unto the eleven as they sat at meat, and upbraided them with their unbelief and hardness of heart, 'because they believed not them which had seen him after he was risen', Mk. 16:14.

And, were it not for his mediatorial work and apostolic power, that unbelief and hardness of heart would have been the end of the gospel. But it was not the end of the gospel. The power of Christ was the end of the gospel.

Just as Mk. 16:8 ends, 'for they were afraid', so Mk. 16:11 ends, 'believed not'. And Mk. 16:13 ends, 'neither believed they them'. Likewise Mk. 16:14 ends, 'believed not them which had seen him after he was risen'. So that the Lord is well used to discovering that wretched unbelief in his own which he must needs overcome to bring them to glory.

This is the destiny of Christ. Raised to sit on the right hand of God, the LORD sends forth the rod of his strength out of Zion. From the womb of the morning he has the dew of his youth. He is possessed of a vigour more than equal to the task of overcoming the unbelief and hardness of heart natural to every one of the heirs of promise.

The report of the appearance of Christ, risen bodily from the dead, was rendered first by Mary to 'them that had been with him', Mk. 16:10; and next by the two to 'the residue', Mk. 16:13. In neither case did the company assembled *necessarily* include the eleven, though they would certainly have heard of the report—and rejected it—from both gatherings.

The appearance 'afterward' to 'the eleven' is most specific. 'Afterward he appeared unto the eleven', Mk. 16:14. A careful reading of Mark's unique record of the appearance *'afterward'* will more than adequately account for any so-called difficulties between Mark and the other gospels.

It is not stated *when* or *where* the Lord 'afterward' appeared to the eleven, Mk. 16:14-18. Presumably whilst still at Jerusalem, and probably on the same first day of the week, thus concluding the threefold witness to the bodily resurrection of Jesus from the dead. This would agree in principle to the earlier visionary witness to the three women.

Doubtless the next reference to 'after', Mk. 16:19—'So then *after* the Lord had spoken unto them'—whilst characteristically abrupt, refers to Galilee, to which the visionary young man had pointed the women, instructing them to tell his disciples, and Peter, that—notwithstanding his previous appearance at Jerusalem—*there* they should see him, Mk. 16:7.

vi. The days following

It was in Galilee that the words of Matthew 28:16-20 were spoken. Mark's *summary*—'So then after the Lord had spoken unto them'—tacitly includes these words recorded in Matthew. But it includes far more. Such an expression must of necessity embrace *all* Jesus' speech, wherever given, up to the time that 'He was received up into heaven'.

Implicitly 'After the Lord had spoken unto them' embraces every word that Jesus spake, by whomsoever recorded, and wherever spoken, whether Galilee, Jerusalem, or Bethany.

No matter that Mark gives neither words, times, nor places: his words *imply* all that is recorded at this period by Matthew, Luke, and John, just as much as the explicit statement of his own narrative. After *that* — *all* that — Mark testifies, 'He was received up into heaven', Mk. 16:19.

From the rich tapestry of the vastly crowded events of this period the Holy Ghost directs Matthew, Mark, Luke, and John to select respectively, each according to purpose.

The vexed carnal mind, so intent upon 'harmony', can neither abide nor fathom the mind of the Spirit in that which is irrelevant to the process of divine revelation. But to the spiritually minded everything is inexpressibly glorious, because glorifying to Christ.

Eager to arrive at the ascension, Mark hastens over much detail, and many events, as if leaping upon the mountains, skipping upon the hills, like to a young hart upon the mountains of Bether. Enraptured by the brightness of the glory of Christ ascended into the heavens, he seems to say, 'Or ever I was aware, my soul made me like the chariots of Amminadib'.

In his ascension the Lord triumphs over all unbelief and hardness of heart, no thanks to man, no, not even despite hearing from them that had *seen* him after he was risen. Therefore the whole power and all the glory in the new testament of necessity *must* belong to the LORD. And *that* is his destiny.

Having upbraided the eleven with their unbelief and hard-ness of heart, the risen Lord gives the first of his charges to the eleven—presumably, but not necessarily, at Jerusalem—as opposed to the next, recorded from Galilee in Matthew. Even then, Mark, consistent with his purpose of exposing the natural unbelief of the flesh *in his own*, stresses of the eleven, 'These signs shall follow *them that believe*', Mk. 16:17.

Jesus charges the eleven to go into all the world and preach the gospel to every creature. Mark that: *the gospel*. This entailed all the truth recorded in Mark, 'the beginning of *the gospel* of Jesus Christ, the Son of God'. That was the commencement.

The epistles bring in the conclusion. Nothing other than this *entire* doctrine is *the gospel*, properly so-called. Nothing else and nothing less than this was to be preached and taught by the eleven. For nothing else and nothing less could save them that believe. The *gospel* of Christ is the power of God unto salvation, Rom. 1:16. Nothing else.

Anything else is spurious. Anything less is false. 'He that *believeth* and is baptized shall be saved.' Then and there. 'But he that *believeth not* shall be damned.' Then and there. The issues of light and darkness are instantaneous and irrevocable in Mark, given the shining forth of the brightness of Christ's glory in the gospel.

As to the signs which should follow them that believe, Mk. 16:17,18, these, attending the preaching of the gospel, applied to 'them', Mk. 16:15. As to 'them', unquestionably it was 'the eleven', Mk. 16:14. But what has that to do with subsequent audacious pretenders to apostolic gifts, such as so-called Pentecostals, or Charismatics? Nothing whatsoever.

Given the remarkable testimony of the early miraculous gifts in the *ecclesia* recorded in Acts, and mentioned in the earliest epistles—such as I Cor. 12—it is equally striking to observe that in later epistles such miraculous signs become conspicuous by their absence.

Thus the historical sequence in the epistles of the various lists of gifts, first in I Cor. 12, then in Rom. 12, and finally in Eph. 4, makes clear the phasing out of exterior signs and wonders in favour of the inward and eternal power of Christ in the preaching of the gospel.

Like the manna, the pillar of fire and cloud, and the water from the rock which followed Israel, after the people were carried over Jordan into their inheritance, the purpose of such miraculous signs had been fulfilled. But the *testimony of the covenant* continued.

Likewise the remarkable miracles attending Peter and the eleven in the Acts. These are not mentioned in the two later epistles of Peter. But if Pentecostals or Charismatics had written I and II Peter, nothing *but* these things would have been mentioned. Where are the early miracles of Acts in the later I, II, or III John? They are not there at all, nor are they mentioned.

What of the wonders wrought by Paul in his early ministry? Where are they in his later writings, or in the pastoral epistles? Having fulfilled their original purpose, the *signs* are not there: but the *thing signified* is there.

What miracles, signs, or wonders were wrought by Timothy or Titus? None. Where are such things in these epistles? Nowhere. But who can equal these faithful followers as successors in the apostolic ministry?

Which of the martyrs made such wildly extravagant claims as these lawless Pentecostals? What Reformer, which Puritan, would not roundly have condemned the Charismatic delusion, and condemned it in the name of Christ and the gospel?

Without exception, all the old divines would have repudiated the impiety of such extravagant pretence with utmost repugnance. And these are the men who laid down their lives that we might receive the word of God unto salvation in Christ Jesus.

The outlandish claims of such pernicious sects — as if *they* could receive what was unique to and given under the apostles — are but comparatively modern novelties. These people, professing — of all things! — the baptism of the Spirit, claim that they can prove it by 'speaking in tongues'.

'They shall speak with new tongues', Mk. 16:17. But that was the eleven. If it is the 'proof' of these people, how come that they were not contemporary with the eleven to whom these words were spoken two thousand years ago?

Oh, but this scripture still applies to them. So they claim. Then let us see their faith—as saith James—by their *works*, as opposed to their *gibberish*. For anyone can lose self-control and babble gibberish. But what of their works? Why not, for example, follow 'they shall speak with new tongues', with 'they shall take up serpents'? Or why not drink 'some deadly thing', Mk. 16:18?

After all, in 1995, one of their number, in a certain American —where else?—State, more rash than those who *merely* raved, brought a rattlesnake in a box to one of their meetings. But why not? 'They shall take up serpents.' To impress his fellows, the man opened the box. The serpent struck immediately, and shortly the man died.

This was not the case with Paul, Acts 28:3-5. But then he was among the apostles. Presumptuous Pentecostals and Charismatics are not. As the dead American demonstrates.

However, if any of them—whoever or wherever they be—are contentious, we propose two simple tests of their honesty. Not their babbling, which cannot be tested, but their works, which can. The first concerns serpents; the second, deadly drink; Mk. 16:18. But, surely, this can give them no problem. For both these apostolic signs follow 'tongues', Mk. 16:17.

How salutary. These two simple tests would rid the world of the vain assumptions of insolent—so-called—Pentecostals and Charismatics, and thus a great service would be rendered to humanity by clearing the truth of the gospel. After all, since these exalted personages apply to themselves the same immunity as the apostles, What have they to fear?

Should not these signs—as well as their claimed new tongues —follow *them* that believe? Then let them appear before us lesser mortals, and, in our presence, drink cyanide, or perhaps arsenic. Let them show us poor shortcomers how to take up a rattlesnake—unlike their dead American fellow-believer—or, it may be, a cobra or so, that we may see their faith by their works.

But enough of these audacious heretics. With what joy those who are of a broken heart and of a contrite spirit, who do not —for they cannot—think of themselves more highly than they ought to think, return to the pure word of the truth of the gospel in the last verses of Mark.

Here the beginning of the gospel of Jesus Christ the Son of God ends as it must. Just as he came down from God out of heaven, appearing so abruptly at the first, as swiftly is he caught up into heaven, ascending to mediate and administer that same new testament which he had declared between the first and the last chapters of the gospel according to Mark.

vii. The Lord's Day

'So then after the Lord had spoken unto them, he was received up into heaven, and sat on the right hand of God.

And they went forth, and preached every where, the Lord working with them, and confirming the word with signs following. Amen.'

The ancient psalmist foresaw these things in the Spirit, saying, 'this is the day which the LORD hath made; we will rejoice and be glad in it.' The same truth appears also in the allegorical significance of 'the first day of the week', Mk. 16:2,9. It is 'the rising of the sun', Mk. 16:2, namely, of 'The Sun of righteousness', which 'shall arise with healing in his beams', Mal. 4:2.

It is evident that the first flush of dawn heralds the beginning of the day, which of necessity continues so long as the sun maintains its ascendancy in the heavens. These things bear witness to 'the day which the LORD hath made', signifying the ascension of the Son of God to the right hand of the Majesty on high.

Of this the patriarch David prophesied over nine hundred years before, declaring that of the fruit of his loins, according to the flesh, God would raise up Christ to sit on his throne. Peter affirms the fulfilment of this word on the day of Pentecost, testifying, 'This Jesus hath God raised up, whereof we all are witnesses'.

'Therefore being by the right hand of God exalted, and having received of the Father the promise of the Holy Ghost, he hath shed forth this, which ye now see and hear.' Thus Christ ascended to sit on the right hand of God.

And this is his destiny in the heavenly glory, throughout the day of the Lord, till he comes again to judge the quick and the dead, according to the word of God in the beginning of the gospel of Jesus Christ, the Son of God. Amen.

JOHN METCALFE

INDEX

TO OTHER PUBLICATIONS

PSALMS, HYMNS AND SPIRITUAL SONGS

THE PSALMS

OF THE

OLD TESTAMENT

The Psalms of the Old Testament, the result of years of painstaking labour, is an original translation into verse from the Authorised Version, which seeks to present the Psalms in the purest scriptural form possible for singing. Here, for the first time, divine names are rendered as and when they occur in the scripture, the distinction between LORD and Lord has been preserved, and every essential point of doctrine and experience appears with unique perception and fidelity.

The Psalms of the Old Testament is the first part of a trilogy written by John Metcalfe, the second part of which is entitled *Spiritual Songs from the Gospels*, and the last, *The Hymns of the New Testament*. These titles provide unique and accurate metrical versions of passages from the psalms, the gospels and the new testament epistles respectively, and are intended to be used together in the worship of God.

Price £2.50 *(postage extra)*
(hard-case binding, dust-jacket)
Printed, sewn and bound
by the John Metcalfe Publishing Trust
ISBN 0 9506366 7 3

SPIRITUAL SONGS

FROM

THE GOSPELS

The *Spiritual Songs from the Gospels*, the result of years of painstaking labour, is an original translation into verse from the Authorised Version, which seeks to present essential parts of the gospels in the purest scriptural form possible for singing. The careful selection from Matthew, Mark, Luke and John, set forth in metrical verse of the highest integrity, enables the singer to sing 'the word of Christ' as if from the scripture itself, 'richly and in all wisdom'; and, above all, in a way that facilitates worship in song of unprecedented fidelity.

The *Spiritual Songs from the Gospels* is the central part of a trilogy written by John Metcalfe, the first part of which is entitled *The Psalms of the Old Testament*, and the last, *The Hymns of the New Testament*. These titles provide unique and accurate metrical versions of passages from the psalms, the gospels and the new testament epistles respectively, and are intended to be used together in the worship of God.

Price £2.50 *(postage extra)*
(hard-case binding, dust-jacket)
Printed, sewn and bound
by the John Metcalfe Publishing Trust
ISBN 0 9506366 8 1

THE HYMNS

OF THE

NEW TESTAMENT

The *Hymns of the New Testament*, the result of years of painstaking labour, is an original translation into verse from the Authorised Version, which presents essential parts of the new testament epistles in the purest scriptural form possible for singing. The careful selection from the book of Acts to that of Revelation, set forth in metrical verse of the highest integrity, enables the singer to sing 'the word of Christ' as if from the scripture itself, 'richly and in all wisdom'; and, above all, in a way that facilitates worship in song of unprecedented fidelity.

The *Hymns of the New Testament* is the last part of a trilogy written by John Metcalfe, the first part of which is entitled *The Psalms of the Old Testament*, and the next, *Spiritual Songs from the Gospels*. These titles provide unique and accurate metrical versions of passages from the psalms, the gospels and the new testament epistles respectively, and are intended to be used together in the worship of God.

Price £2.50 *(postage extra)*
(hard-case binding, dust-jacket)
Printed, sewn and bound
by the John Metcalfe Publishing Trust
ISBN 0 9506366 9 X

vii

'THE APOSTOLIC FOUNDATION
OF THE
CHRISTIAN CHURCH' SERIES

x

Third Printing

FOUNDATIONS UNCOVERED

THE APOSTOLIC FOUNDATION
OF THE
CHRISTIAN CHURCH

Volume I

Foundations Uncovered is the introduction to the major series: 'The Apostolic Foundation of the Christian Church'.

Rich in truth, the Introduction deals comprehensively with the foundation of the apostolic faith under the descriptive titles: The Word, The Doctrine, The Truth, The Gospel, The Faith, The New Testament, and The Foundation.

The contents of the book reveal: The Fact of the Foundation; The Foundation Uncovered; What the Foundation is not; How the Foundation is Described; and, Being Built upon the Foundation.

'This book comes with the freshness of a new Reformation.'

Price 75p *(postage extra)*
(Laminated cover)
Printed, sewn and bound
by the John Metcalfe Publishing Trust
ISBN 0 9506366 5 7

Thoroughly revised and extensively rewritten
second edition

Third Printing

THE BIRTH OF JESUS CHRIST

THE APOSTOLIC FOUNDATION
OF THE
CHRISTIAN CHURCH

Volume II

'The very spirit of adoration and worship rings through the pages of *The Birth of Jesus Christ.*

'The author expresses with great clarity the truths revealed to him in his study of holy scriptures at depth. We are presented here with a totally lofty view of the Incarnation.

'John Metcalfe is to be classed amongst the foremost expositors of our age; and his writings have about them that quality of timelessness that makes me sure they will one day take their place among the heritage of truly great Christian works.'

From a review by Rev. David Catterson.

'Uncompromisingly faithful to scripture ... has much to offer which is worth serious consideration ... deeply moving.'

The Expository Times.

Price 95p *(postage extra)*
(Laminated Cover)
Printed, sewn and bound
by the John Metcalfe Publishing Trust
ISBN 1 870039 48 3

*Thoroughly revised and extensively rewritten
second edition (Hardback)*

Third Printing

THE MESSIAH

THE APOSTOLIC FOUNDATION
OF THE
CHRISTIAN CHURCH

Volume III

The Messiah is a spiritually penetrating and entirely original exposition of Matthew chapter one to chapter seven from the trenchant pen of John Metcalfe.

Matthew Chapters One to Seven

GENEALOGY · BIRTH · STAR OF BETHLEHEM
HEROD · FLIGHT TO EGYPT · NAZARETH
JOHN THE BAPTIST · THE BAPTIST'S MINISTRY
JESUS' BAPTISM · ALL RIGHTEOUSNESS FULFILLED
HEAVEN OPENED · THE SPIRIT'S DESCENT
THE TEMPTATION OF JESUS IN THE WILDERNESS
JESUS' MANIFESTATION · THE CALLING · THE TRUE DISCIPLES
THE BEATITUDES · THE SERMON ON THE MOUNT

'Something of the fire of the ancient Hebrew prophet .... Metcalfe has spiritual and expository potentials of a high order.'

The Life of Faith.

Price £7.75 *(postage extra)*
Hardback 420 pages
Laminated bookjacket
Printed, sewn and bound
by the John Metcalfe Publishing Trust
ISBN 1 870039 51 3

Second Edition (Hardback)

THE SON OF GOD AND SEED OF DAVID

THE APOSTOLIC FOUNDATION
OF THE
CHRISTIAN CHURCH

Volume IV

The Son of God and Seed of David is the fourth volume in the major work entitled 'The Apostolic Foundation of the Christian Church.'

'The author proceeds to open and allege that Jesus Christ is and ever was *The Son of God*. This greatest of subjects, this most profound of all mysteries, is handled with reverence and with outstanding perception.

'The second part considers *The Seed of David*. What is meant precisely by 'the seed'? And why 'of David'? With prophetic insight the author expounds these essential verities.'

Price £6.95 *(postage extra)*
Hardback 250 pages
Laminated bookjacket
Printed, sewn and bound
by the John Metcalfe Publishing Trust
ISBN 1 870039 16 5

CHRIST CRUCIFIED

THE APOSTOLIC FOUNDATION
OF THE
CHRISTIAN CHURCH

Volume V

Christ Crucified the definitive work on the crucifixion, the blood, and the cross of Jesus Christ.

The crucifixion of Jesus Christ witnessed in the Gospels: the gospel according to Matthew; Mark; Luke; John.

The blood of Jesus Christ declared in the Epistles: the shed blood; the blood of purchase; redemption through his blood; the blood of sprinkling; the blood of the covenant.

The doctrine of the cross revealed in the apostolic foundation of the Christian church: the doctrine of the cross; the cross and the body of sin; the cross and the carnal mind; the cross and the law; the offence of the cross; the cross of our Lord Jesus Christ.

Price £6.95 *(postage extra)*
Hardback 300 pages
Laminated bookjacket
Printed, sewn and bound
by the John Metcalfe Publishing Trust
ISBN 1 870039 08 4

JUSTIFICATION BY FAITH

THE APOSTOLIC FOUNDATION
OF THE
CHRISTIAN CHURCH

Volume VI

THE HEART OF THE GOSPEL · THE FOUNDATION OF THE CHURCH
THE ISSUE OF ETERNITY
CLEARLY, ORIGINALLY AND POWERFULLY OPENED

The basis · The righteousness of the law
The righteousness of God · The atonement · Justification
Traditional views considered · Righteousness imputed to faith
Faith counted for righteousness · Justification by Faith

'And it came to pass, when Jesus had ended these sayings, the people
were astonished at his doctrine: for he taught them as one having
authority, and not as the scribes.' Matthew 7:28,29.

Price £7.50 (postage extra)
Hardback 375 pages
Laminated bookjacket
Printed, sewn and bound
by the John Metcalfe Publishing Trust
ISBN 1870039 11 4

THE CHURCH: WHAT IS IT?

THE APOSTOLIC FOUNDATION
OF THE
CHRISTIAN CHURCH

Volume VII

The answer to this question proceeds first from the lips of Jesus himself, Mt. 16:18, later to be expounded by the words of the apostles whom he sent.

Neither fear of man nor favour from the world remotely affect the answer.

Here is the truth, the whole truth, and nothing but the truth.

The complete originality, the vast range, and the total fearlessness of this book command the attention in a way that is unique.

Read this book: you will never read another like it.

Outspokenly devastating yet devastatingly constructive.

Price £7.75 (postage extra)
Hardback 400 pages
Laminated bookjacket
Printed, sewn and bound
by the John Metcalfe Publishing Trust
ISBN 1 870039 23 8

xvii

xviii

OTHER TITLES

NOAH AND THE FLOOD

Noah and the Flood expounds with vital urgency the man and the message that heralded the end of the old world. The description of the flood itself is vividly realistic. The whole work has an unmistakable ring of authority, and speaks as 'Thus saith the Lord'.

'Mr. Metcalfe makes a skilful use of persuasive eloquence as he challenges the reality of one's profession of faith ... he gives a rousing call to a searching self-examination and evaluation of one's spiritual experience.'

The Monthly Record of the Free Church of Scotland.

Price £1.90 *(postage extra)*
(Laminated Cover)
Printed, sewn and bound
by the John Metcalfe Publishing Trust
ISBN 1 870039 22 X

DIVINE FOOTSTEPS

Divine Footsteps traces the pathway of the feet of the Son of man from the very beginning in the prophetic figures of the true in the old testament through the reality in the new; doing so in a way of experimental spirituality. At the last a glimpse of the coming glory is beheld as his feet are viewed as standing at the latter day upon the earth.

Price 95p *(postage extra)*
(Laminated Cover)
Printed, sewn and bound
by the John Metcalfe Publishing Trust
ISBN 1 870039 21 1

THE RED HEIFER

The Red Heifer was the name given to a sacrifice used by the children of Israel in the Old Testament—as recorded in Numbers 19—in which a heifer was slain and burned. Cedar wood, hyssop and scarlet were cast into the burning, and the ashes were mingled with running water and put in a vessel. It was kept for the children of Israel for a water of separation: it was a purification for sin.

In this unusual book the sacrifice is brought up to date and its relevance to the church today is shown.

Price 75p (*postage extra*)
ISBN 0 9502515 4 2

THE WELLS OF SALVATION

The Wells of Salvation is written from a series of seven powerful addresses preached at Tylers Green. It is a forthright and experimental exposition of Isaiah 12:3, 'Therefore with joy shall ye draw water out of the wells of salvation.'

John Metcalfe is acknowledged to be perhaps the most gifted expositor and powerful preacher of our day and this is to be seen clearly in The Wells of Salvation.

Price £1.50 (*postage extra*)
(Laminated Cover)
ISBN 0 9502515 6 9

OF GOD OR MAN?

LIGHT FROM GALATIANS

The Epistle to the Galatians contends for deliverance from the law and from carnal ministry.

The Apostle opens his matter in two ways:

Firstly, Paul vindicates himself and his ministry against those that came not from God above, but from Jerusalem below.

Secondly, he defends the Gospel and evangelical liberty against legal perversions and bondage to the flesh.

Price £1.45 *(postage extra)*
(Laminated Cover)
ISBN 0 9506366 3 0

A QUESTION FOR POPE JOHN PAUL II

As a consequence of his many years spent apart in prayer, lonely vigil, and painstaking study of the scripture, John Metcalfe asks a question and looks for an answer from Pope John Paul II.

Price £1.25. *(postage extra)*
(Laminated Cover)
ISBN 0 9506366 4 9

THE BOOK OF RUTH

The Book of Ruth is set against the farming background of old testament Israel at the time of the Judges, the narrative—unfolding the work of God in redemption—being marked by a series of agricultural events.

These events—the famine; the barley harvest; the wheat harvest; the winnowing—possessed a hidden spiritual significance to that community, but, much more, they speak in figure directly to our own times, as the book reveals.

Equally contemporary appear the characters of Ruth, Naomi, Boaz, and the first kinsman, drawn with spiritual perception greatly to the profit of the reader.

Price £4.95 *(postage extra)*
Hardback 200 pages
Laminated bookjacket
Printed, sewn and bound
by the John Metcalfe Publishing Trust
ISBN 1 870039 17 3

PRESENT-DAY CONVERSIONS
OF THE NEW TESTAMENT KIND

FROM THE MINISTRY OF

JOHN METCALFE

The outstandingly striking presentation of this fascinating paperback will surely catch the eye, as its title and contents will certainly captivate the mind: here is a unique publication.

Woven into a gripping narrative, over twenty-one short life stories, all centred on conversions that simply could not have happened had not God broken in, and had not Christ been revealed, the book presents a tremendous challenge, at once moving and thrilling to the reader.

Price £2.25 *(postage extra)*
(Laminated Cover)
Printed, sewn and bound
by the John Metcalfe Publishing Trust
ISBN 1 870039 31 9

DIVINE MEDITATIONS

OF

WILLIAM HUNTINGTON

Originally published by Mr. Huntington as a series of letters to J. Jenkins, under the title of 'Contemplations on the God of Israel', the spiritual content of this correspondence has been skilfully and sympathetically edited, abridged, and arranged so as to form a series of meditations, suitable for daily readings.

Mr. Huntington's own text is thereby adapted to speak directly to the reader in a way much more suited to his ministering immediately to ourselves, in our own circumstances and times.

It is greatly hoped that many today will benefit from this adaption which carefully retains both the spirit and the letter of the text. If any prefer the original format, this is readily available from several sources and many libraries.

Nevertheless, the publishers believe the much more readable form into which Mr. Huntington's very words have been adapted will appeal to a far wider audience, for whose comfort and consolation this carefully edited work has been published.

Price £2.35 (*postage extra*)
(Laminated Cover)
Printed, sewn and bound
by the John Metcalfe Publishing Trust
ISBN 1 870039 24 6

SAVING FAITH

The sevenfold work of the Holy Ghost in bringing a sinner to saving faith in Christ opened and enlarged.

True faith is the work of God. False faith is the presumption of man. But where is the difference? *Saving Faith* shows the difference.

Price £2.25 *(postage extra)*
Paperback 250 pages
(Laminated Cover)
Printed, sewn and bound
by the John Metcalfe Publishing Trust
ISBN 1 870039 40 8

DELIVERANCE FROM THE LAW
THE WESTMINSTER CONFESSION EXPLODED

Deliverance from the law. A devastating vindication of the gospel of Christ against the traditions of man.

Price £1.90 *(postage extra)*
Paperback 160 pages
(Laminated Cover)
Printed, sewn and bound
by the John Metcalfe Publishing Trust
ISBN 1 870039 41 6

THE BEATITUDES

A unique insight destined to be the classic opening of this wonderful sequence of utterances from the lips of Jesus.

The reader will discover a penetration of the spiritual heights and divine depths of these peerless words in a way ever fresh and always rewarding though read time and time again.

Price £1.90 *(postage extra)*
Paperback 185 pages
(Laminated cover)
Printed, sewn and bound
by the John Metcalfe Publishing Trust
ISBN 1 870039 45 9

NEWLY PUBLISHED
COLOSSIANS

This concise and unique revelation of the Epistle to the
Colossians has the hallmark of spiritual originality and insight
peculiar to the ministry of John Metcalfe. It is as if a diamond,
inert and lifeless in itself, has been divinely cut at great cost, so
that every way in which it is turned, the light from above is
enhanced and magnified to break forth with divine radiance
showing colour and depth hitherto unsuspected.

The Trustees give glory and thanks to God for the privilege of
producing and subsidising this work.

Price 95p *(postage extra)*
Paperback 135 pages
(Laminated cover)
Printed, sewn and bound
by the John Metcalfe Publishing Trust
ISBN 1 870039 55 6

NEWLY PUBLISHED

PHILIPPIANS

The Epistle of Paul the Apostle to the Philippians is opened
by this work from the pen of John Metcalfe with that lucid
thoroughness which one has come to expect from a ministry
received 'not of men, neither by man, but by the revelation of
Jesus Christ'.

The work of God at Philippi is traced 'from the first day' until
the time at which the epistle was written. Never were Lydia
or the Philippian jailor drawn with more lively insight. The
epistle itself is revealed in order, with passages—such as 'the
mind that was in Christ Jesus'—that evidence the work of no
less than a divine for our own times.

The Trustees give glory and thanks to God for the privilege
of producing and subsidising this book.

Price £1.90 *(postage extra)*
Paperback 185 pages
(Laminated cover)
Printed, sewn and bound
by the John Metcalfe Publishing Trust
ISBN 1 870039 56 4

NEWLY PUBLISHED
FIRST TIMOTHY

This penetrating revelation of the first epistle to Timothy opens the substance of five consecutive lectures given by John Metcalfe in The Hoare Memorial Hall, Church House, Westminster, London.

The Trustees give glory and thanks to God for the privilege of producing and subsidising this work.

Price £2.00 *(postage extra)*
Paperback 220 pages
(Laminated Cover)
Printed, sewn and bound
by the John Metcalfe Publishing Trust
ISBN 1 870039 67 X

'TRACT FOR THE TIMES' SERIES

'TRACT FOR THE TIMES' SERIES

The Gospel of God by John Metcalfe. No. 1 in the Series. Laminated Cover, price 25p.

The Strait Gate by John Metcalfe. No. 2 in the Series. Laminated Cover, price 25p.

Eternal Sonship and Taylor Brethren by John Metcalfe. No. 3 in the Series. Laminated Cover, price 25p.

Marks of the New Testament Church by John Metcalfe. No. 4 in the Series. Laminated Cover, price 25p.

The Charismatic Delusion by John Metcalfe. No. 5 in the Series. Laminated Cover, price 25p.

Premillennialism Exposed by John Metcalfe. No. 6 in the Series. Laminated Cover, price 25p.

Justification and Peace by John Metcalfe. No. 7 in the Series. Laminated Cover, price 25p.

Faith or Presumption? by John Metcalfe. No. 8 in the Series. Laminated Cover, price 25p.

The Elect Undeceived by John Metcalfe. No. 9 in the Series. Laminated Cover, price 25p.

Justifying Righteousness by John Metcalfe. No. 10 in the Series. Laminated Cover, price 25p.

Righteousness Imputed by John Metcalfe. No. 11 in the Series. Laminated Cover, price 25p.

The Great Deception by John Metcalfe. No. 12 in the Series. Laminated Cover, price 25p.

A Famine in the Land by John Metcalfe. No. 13 in the Series. Laminated Cover, price 25p.

Blood and Water by John Metcalfe. No. 14 in the Series. Laminated Cover, price 25p.

Women Bishops? by John Metcalfe. No. 15 in the Series. Laminated Cover, price 25p.

The Heavenly Vision by John Metcalfe. No. 16 in the Series. Laminated Cover, price 25p.

EVANGELICAL TRACTS

EVANGELICAL TRACTS

1. **The Two Prayers of Elijah.** Green card cover, price 10p.

2. **Wounded for our Transgressions.** Gold card cover, price 10p.

3. **The Blood of Sprinkling.** Red card cover, price 10p.

4. **The Grace of God that brings Salvation.** Blue card cover, price 10p.

5. **The Name of Jesus.** Rose card cover, price 10p.

6. **The Ministry of the New Testament.** Purple card cover, price 10p.

7. **The Death of the Righteous** (*The closing days of J.B. Stoney*) by A.M.S. (his daughter). Ivory card cover, Price 10p.

8. **Repentance.** Sky blue card cover, price 10p.

9. **Legal Deceivers Exposed.** Crimson card cover, price 10p.

10. **Unconditional Salvation.** Green card cover, price 10p.

11. **Religious Merchandise.** Brown card cover, price 10p.

12. **Comfort.** Pink card cover, price 10p.

13. **Peace.** Grey card cover, price 10p.

14. **Eternal Life.** Cobalt card cover, price 10p.

15. **The Handwriting of Ordinances.** Fawn card cover, price 10p.

16. **'Lord, Lord!'.** Emerald card cover, price 10p.

ECCLESIA TRACTS

ECCLESIA TRACTS

The Beginning of the Ecclesia by John Metcalfe. No. 1 in the Series, Sand grain cover, Price 10p.

Churches and the Church by J.N. Darby. Edited. No. 2 in the Series, Sand grain cover, Price 10p.

The Ministers of Christ by John Metcalfe. No. 3 in the Series, Sand grain cover, Price 10p.

The Inward Witness by George Fox. Edited. No. 4 in the Series, Sand grain cover, Price 10p.

The Notion of a Clergyman by J.N. Darby. Edited. No. 5 in the Series, Sand grain cover, Price 10p.

The Servant of the Lord by William Huntington. Edited and Abridged. No. 6 in the Series, Sand grain cover, Price 10p.

One Spirit by William Kelly. Edited. No. 7 in the Series, Sand grain cover, Price 10p.

The Funeral of Arminianism by William Huntington. Edited and Abridged. No. 8 in the Series, Sand grain cover, Price 10p.

One Body by William Kelly. Edited. No. 9 in the Series, Sand grain cover, Price 10p.

False Churches and True by John Metcalfe. No. 10 in the Series, Sand grain cover, Price 10p.

Separation from Evil by J.N. Darby. Edited. No. 11 in the Series, Sand grain cover, Price 10p.

The Remnant by J.B. Stoney. Edited. No. 12 in the Series, Sand grain cover, Price 10p.

The Arminian Skeleton by William Huntington. Edited and Abridged. No. 13 in the Series, Sand grain cover, Price 10p.

FOUNDATION TRACTS

FOUNDATION TRACTS

1. **Female Priests?** by John Metcalfe. Oatmeal cover, price 25p.

2. **The Bondage of the Will** by Martin Luther. Translated and Abridged. Oatmeal cover, price 25p.

3. **Of the Popish Mass** by John Calvin. Translated and Abridged. Oatmeal cover, price 25p.

4. **The Adversary** by John Metcalfe. Oatmeal cover, price 25p.

5. **The Advance of Popery** by J.C. Philpot. Oatmeal cover, price 25p.

6. **Enemies in the Land** by John Metcalfe. Oatmeal cover, price 25p.

7. **An Admonition Concerning Relics** by John Calvin. Oatmeal cover, price 25p.

8. **John Metcalfe's Testimony Against Falsity in Worship** by John Metcalfe. Oatmeal cover, price 25p.

9. **Brethrenism Exposed** by John Metcalfe. Oatmeal cover, price 25p.

10. **John Metcalfe's Testimony Against The Social Gospel** by John Metcalfe. Oatmeal cover, price 25p.

1

MINISTRY BY JOHN METCALFE

TAPE MINISTRY BY JOHN METCALFE
FROM ENGLAND AND THE FAR EAST
IS AVAILABLE.

In order to obtain this free recorded ministry, please send your
blank cassette (C.90) and the cost of the return postage, including
your name and address in block capitals, to the John Metcalfe
Publishing Trust, Church Road, Tylers Green, Penn, Bucks,
HP10 8LN. Tapelists are available on request.

**Owing to the increased demand for the tape ministry, we are unable to
supply more than two tapes per order, except in the case of meetings for
the hearing of tapes, where a special arrangement can be made.**

lii

THE MINISTRY OF THE NEW TESTAMENT

The purpose of this substantial A4 gloss paper magazine is to provide spiritual and experimental ministry with sound doctrine which rightly and prophetically divides the Word of Truth.

Readers of our books will already know the high standards of our publications. They can be confident that these pages will maintain that quality, by giving access to enduring ministry from the past, much of which is derived from sources that are virtually unobtainable today, and publishing a living ministry from the present. Selected articles from the following writers have already been included:

ELI ASHDOWN · JOHN BERRIDGE · ABRAHAM BOOTH
JOHN BRADFORD · JOHN BUNYAN · JOHN BURGON
JOHN CALVIN · DONALD CARGILL · JOHN CENNICK · J.N. DARBY
GEORGE FOX · JOHN FOXE · WILLIAM GADSBY · JOHN GUTHRIE
WILLIAM GUTHRIE · GREY HAZLERIGG · WILLIAM HUNTINGTON
WILLIAM KELLY · JOHN KENNEDY · JOHN KERSHAW
JOHN KEYT · HANSERD KNOLLYS · JOHN KNOX · JAMES LEWIS
MARTIN LUTHER · ROBERT MURRAY MCCHEYNE · JOHN METCALFE
ALEXANDER—SANDY—PEDEN · J.C. PHILPOT · J.K. POPHAM
JAMES RENWICK · J.B. STONEY · HENRY TANNER
ARTHUR TRIGGS · JOHN VINALL · JOHN WARBURTON
JOHN WELWOOD · GEORGE WHITEFIELD · J.A. WYLIE

Price £1.75 *(postage included)*
Issued Spring, Summer, Autumn, Winter.

Book Order Form

Please send to the address below:-

	Price	Quantity
	Price	Quantity
A Question for Pope John Paul II	£1.25	......
Of God or Man?	£1.45	......
Noah and the Flood	£1.90	......
Divine Footsteps	£0.95	......
The Red Heifer	£0.75	......
The Wells of Salvation	£1.50	......
The Book of Ruth (Hardback edition)	£4.95	......
Divine Meditations of William Huntington	£2.35	......
Present-Day Conversions of the New Testament Kind	£2.25	......
Saving Faith	£2.25	......
Deliverance from the Law	£1.90	......
The Beatitudes	£1.90	......
Colossians	£0.95	......
Philippians	£1.90	......
Matthew	£0.95	......
Philemon	£1.90	......
First Timothy	£2.00	......
Mark	£2.35	......

Psalms, Hymns & Spiritual Songs (Hardback edition)

	Price	Quantity
The Psalms of the Old Testament	£2.50	......
Spiritual Songs from the Gospels	£2.50	......
The Hymns of the New Testament	£2.50	......

'Apostolic Foundation of the Christian Church' series

		Price	Quantity
Foundations Uncovered	Vol.I	£0.75	......
The Birth of Jesus Christ	Vol.II	£0.95	......
The Messiah (Hardback edition)	Vol.III	£7.75	......
The Son of God and Seed of David (Hardback edition)	Vol.IV	£6.95	......
Christ Crucified (Hardback edition)	Vol.V	£6.95	......
Justification by Faith (Hardback edition)	Vol.VI	£7.50	......
The Church: What is it? (Hardback edition)	Vol.VII	£7.75	......

Name and Address (in block capitals)

. . . .

. . . .

. . . .

If money is sent with order please allow for postage. Please address to:- The John Metcalfe Publishing Trust, Church Road, Tylers Green, Penn, Bucks, HP10 8LN.

Tract Order Form

Please send to the address below:-

		Price	Quantity
Evangelical Tracts			
The Two Prayers of Elijah		£0.10	......
Wounded for our Transgressions		£0.10	......
The Blood of Sprinkling		£0.10	......
The Grace of God that Brings Salvation		£0.10	......
The Name of Jesus		£0.10	......
The Ministry of the New Testament		£0.10	......
The Death of the Righteous by A.M.S.		£0.10	......
Repentance		£0.10	......
Legal Deceivers Exposed		£0.10	......
Unconditional Salvation		£0.10	......
Religious Merchandise		£0.10	......
Comfort		£0.10	......
Peace		£0.10	......
Eternal Life		£0.10	......
The Handwriting of Ordinances		£0.10	......
'Lord, Lord!'		£0.10	......
'Tract for the Times' series			
The Gospel of God	No.1	£0.25	......
The Strait Gate	No.2	£0.25	......
Eternal Sonship and Taylor Brethren	No.3	£0.25	......
Marks of the New Testament Church	No.4	£0.25	......
The Charismatic Delusion	No.5	£0.25	......
Premillennialism Exposed	No.6	£0.25	......
Justification and Peace	No.7	£0.25	......
Faith or presumption?	No.8	£0.25	......
The Elect undeceived	No.9	£0.25	......
Justifying Righteousness	No.10	£0.25	......
Righteousness Imputed	No.11	£0.25	......
The Great Deception	No.12	£0.25	......
A Famine in the Land	No.13	£0.25	......
Blood and Water	No.14	£0.25	......
Women Bishops?	No.15	£0.25	......
The Heavenly Vision	No.16	£0.25	......

Name and Address (in block capitals)

. . . .

. . . .

. . . .

If money is sent with order please allow for postage. Please address to:- The
John Metcalfe Publishing Trust, Church Road, Tylers Green, Penn, Bucks, HP10 8LN.

Tract Order Form

Please send to the address below:-

		Price	Quantity
Ecclesia Tracts			
The Beginning of the Ecclesia	No.1	£0.10	......
Churches and the Church (J.N.D.)	No.2	£0.10	......
The Ministers of Christ	No.3	£0.10	......
The Inward Witness (G.F.)	No.4	£0.10	......
The Notion of a Clergyman (J.N.D.)	No.5	£0.10	......
The Servant of the Lord (W.H.)	No.6	£0.10	......
One Spirit (W.K.)	No.7	£0.10	......
The Funeral of Arminianism (W.H.)	No.8	£0.10	......
One Body (W.K.)	No.9	£0.10	......
False Churches and True	No.10	£0.10	......
Separation from Evil (J.N.D.)	No.11	£0.10	......
The Remnant (J.B.S.)	No.12	£0.10	......
The Arminian Skeleton (W.H.)	No.13	£0.10	......
Foundation Tracts			
Female Priests?	No.1	£0.25	......
The Bondage of the Will (Martin Luther)	No.2	£0.25	......
Of the Popish Mass (John Calvin)	No.3	£0.25	......
The Adversary	No.4	£0.25	......
The Advance of Popery (J.C. Philpot)	No.5	£0.25	......
Enemies in the Land	No.6	£0.25	......
An Admonition Concerning Relics (John Calvin)	No.7	£0.25	......
John Metcalfe's Testimony Against Falsity in Worship	No.8	£0.25	......
Brethrenism Exposed	No.9	£0.25	......
John Metcalfe's Testimony Against The Social Gospel	No.10	£0.25	......

Name and Address (in block capitals)

. . . .

. . . .

. . . .

If money is sent with order please allow for postage. Please address to:- The
John Metcalfe Publishing Trust, Church Road, Tylers Green, Penn, Bucks, HP10 8LN.

Magazine Order Form

Name and Address (in block capitals)

. . . .

. . . .

. . . .

Please send me .... current copy/copies of The Ministry of the New Testament.

Please send me .... year/s subscription.

I enclose a cheque/postal order for £ ....

(Price: including postage, U.K. £1.75; Overseas £1.90)
(One year's subscription: Including postage, U.K. £7.00; Overseas £7.60)

Cheques should be made payable to The John Metcalfe Publishing Trust, and for overseas subscribers should be in pounds sterling drawn on a London Bank.

10 or more copies to one address will qualify for a 10% discount

Back numbers from Spring 1986 available.

Please send to The John Metcalfe Publishing Trust, Church Road, Tylers Green, Penn, Bucks, HP10 8LN

All Publications of the Trust are subsidised by the Publishers.